CULTS AND NONCONVENTIONAL RELIGIOUS GROUPS

A COLLECTION
OF OUTSTANDING STUDIES
AND MONOGRAPHS

edited by

J. GORDON MELTON
INSTITUTE FOR THE STUDY
OF AMERICAN RELIGION

A GARLAND SERIES

A HISTORY
OF THE UNIFICATION
CHURCH IN AMERICA
1959–1974

EMERGENCE OF A NATIONAL MOVEMENT

MICHAEL L. MICKLER

GARLAND PUBLISHING, INC.
NEW YORK & LONDON / 1993

Copyright © 1993 by Michael L. Mickler
All rights reserved

Library of Congress Cataloging-in-Publication Data

Mickler, Michael L., 1949–.
    A history of the Unification Church in America, 1959–1974 : emer-
gence of a national movement / by Michael L. Mickler.
        p.   cm. — (Cults and nonconventional religious groups)
    Includes bibliographical references (p. xxx-xxx) and index.
    ISBN 0–8153–1138–9 (alk. paper)
    1. Unification Church—United States—History.   2. United States—
Church history—20th century.   I. Title.   II. Series.
BX9750.S43M53   1993
289.9'6'0973—dc20   93–27146
                                                                           CIP

Printed on acid-free, 250-year-life paper
Manufactured in the United States of America

To My Parents

CONTENTS

PREFACE   ix

CHAPTER ONE: BEGINNINGS   3

    Miss Kim Joins the Movement—The Mission to
    Oregon—Flight to San Francisco

CHAPTER TWO: TO THE BAY AREA: 1960–63   15

    The Community—Visa Problems—From
    Community to Corporation—Improving the
    Text—Friends and Foes—Spreading the
    Word—Bay Area and Beyond—The
    Newsletter—Circuit Rider—Training Session
    Crisis—Success

CHAPTER THREE: EXODUS : 1964–65   59

    Local Changes—Prediction of Economic
    Collapse—Sir Anthony Brooke—Community
    Style— Rev. Moon Visits America—The World
    Tour—Back to the Bay Area

CHAPTER FOUR: THE RE-EDUCATION
                  FOUNDATION: 1966–71   87

*Mr. Choi Joins the Movement—The Mission to
Japan— Early Days in San Francisco—The
Re-Education Center—International Exchange
Press—The Principles of Education—Founding
the International Ideal City—The International
Re-Education Foundation—The International
Pioneer Academy—International Friendship
Banquets-Final Success*

CHAPTER FIVE: A NATIONAL MOVEMENT
               ATTEMPTS TO EMERGE: 1966–71   133

*A National Movement Attempts to Emerge-The
Berkeley Center—Rev. Moon's Second World
Tour—Reconsolidation—United Faith, Inc.*

CHAPTER SIX: A NATIONAL MOVEMENT
                EMERGES: 1972–74   173

*The Third World Tour—One World
Crusade—Mobile Fundraising Teams—First
ICUS Conference—Meeting the Politicos—A
National Movement Emerges—Madison Square
Garden—The Time Bomb Is Ticking—Success
in San Francisco—The Oakland Family*

INDEX   221

PREFACE

This study recounts the earliest beginnings of the Unification Church in America. Although now recognized as a strongly centralized movement, during the 1960s the church consisted of three separately-incorporated missionary groupings each with disparate methods of proselytization, differing interpretations of doctrine, and distinctive organizational styles. Two of these groups directed fluctuating networks of 'centers' throughout the country. All of them maintained a presence in the San Francisco Bay Area which became a focal point for their potential unification. What, in fact, emerged was a complicated set of missionary jurisdictions, strategic alliances, and general grievances, nowhere more focused than in the Bay Area.

Besides describing these groups and their unsuccessful efforts to forge unity during the 1960s, the study details factors which led to the emergence of a national movement during the early 1970s. The most significant of these was the presence in America of Rev. Moon. By 1974, each of the earlier missionary groupings was non-existent. However, certain of their emphases survived within the "Oakland Family" which during the mid and late 1970s emerged alongside the national structure as an alternative tradition.

As the first published history of the Unification Church in America, this work is intended neither as a sociological or theological analysis nor as an apology or critique of the church. Rather, it is intended as a historical account of the church's origins and development in America during a fifteen-year period from the first arrival of Korean missionaries in 1959 to the establishment of a viable national movement in 1974. After 1974, the movement's rapid growth, perceived ambitions and alleged deviance provoked negative reactions. These included media attacks, kidnappings of members, deprogrammings, government investigations, court cases, and ultimately the incarceration of Rev. Moon. However, as these events unfolded outside the chronological framework of this account, they will be addressed in a forthcoming volume. Again, the intent of this work is not to justify, criticize or defend. The sole attempt is to document, as closely as possible, the rise and early development of the Unification Church in America.

Although I have attempted to be comprehensive in highlighting the dominant personalities, organizations and circumstances which facilitated the emergence of a national movement, this work does not cover everything. Most notably, it does not deal with numerous regional or local initiatives which did not directly figure into the emergent national structure. To this extent, the account intentionally focuses on the movement's mainstream development. Another study, with altered emphases, might well reconstruct a decidedly different story.

A couple of notes on sources. Because a historical account of the movement has not been compiled, this study makes use of sources not previously utilized, some of which are not published. The bulk of these are church materials: periodicals, books, memoirs, brochures, prospectuses, letters, diaries and the like. Many of these materials are not easily accessible although repositories include Unification Theological Seminary, Barrytown, New York; Unification Church of America National Headquarters, New York City; the New Religious Movement Collection at the Graduate Theological Union Library, Berkeley, California; and the files of the Institute for the Study of American Religion (ISAR) now housed at the University of California at Santa Barbara.

Where possible, I have attempted to corroborate movement accounts with outside sources although the church was not widely known prior to the early 1970s. The only substantial study of the movement during the 1960s is John Lofland's *Doomsday Cult* (Prentice-Hall, 1966) which analyses the earliest church community in the San Francisco Bay Area. Although

Lofland employed pseudonyms and professed greater interest in sociological questions than in the movement, his treatment is an important source of data and is cited extensively in this work's initial two chapters. Subsequent chapters contain additional references, mainly to newspaper accounts. Apart from print sources, I conducted a number of interviews some of which are noted in the text's citations.

This study could not have been undertaken or completed without the assistance of a number of persons. Since it began as a thesis, I'd first like to thank my academic advisors: Dr. J. Stillson Judah, Dr. Lewis Rambo, and especially Dr. Elden Ernst whose historical expertise is responsible for any wider appeal this work may have. I also wish to thank Dr. A. Durwood Foster and Dr. Richard Quebedeaux. Special thanks are due to the many Unification Church members who loaned me materials, granted personal interviews and lived with me during the research and writing of this history. I am especially grateful to the late Dr. Young Oon Kim who granted me several interviews and access to her as yet unpublished memoirs; Mr. Sang Ik Choi who opened his home to me on several occasions for extended interviews; and Dr. David S.C. Kim and his family for their support. I'd also like to thank Dr. and Mrs. Mose Durst for their cooperation, Mrs. Joy Pople who typed the original manuscript, and Mr. Michael Balcomb for his very able editorial and technical assistance in preparing this work for publication.

Michael L. Mickler
Barrytown, New York
November 1993

A History
of the Unification
Church in America
1959–1974

CHAPTER ONE

BEGINNINGS

Miss Kim Joins the Movement — The Mission to Oregon
Flight to San Francisco

A history of the Unification Church in America, like most histories, is somewhat determined by where one begins. If, for example, one begins with the establishment of the "Holy Spirit Association for the Unification of World Christianity" (HSA-UWC), as the Unification Church is formally known, in Seoul, Korea on May 1, 1954, and follows the church through the cities and villages of South Korea during the 1950s, to Japan in 1958, and to America in 1959, the history is one of missionary expansion. If, on the other hand, one begins with the church's early January 1959 arrival in the United States and follows its adaptation to and experimentation within that setting, the history is equally that of the culturally conditioning and potentially transforming influences of American national life.

Both of these starting points are important and will be taken into account. However, this treatment will opt for a third and, perhaps, mediating beginning in the person of Young Oon Kim. Having joined the church in 1954, Miss Kim was the first Unification Church missionary to America and she, more than anyone else, shaped the character of its earliest community. In this sense, a history of the Unification Church in America begins with her story.

3

Miss Kim Joins the Movement

Unfortunately, the printed sources relating to Miss Kim's life before joining the church and her early days in the church are limited. The most important are her memoirs (unpublished) and a transcribed testimony delivered in Sacramento, California, July 24, 1963. Nonetheless, these contain relevant biographical detail which can be grouped under the headings of formative influences, conversion and mission.

Formative influences

The most obvious formative influence on Miss Kim's early life was the Christian religion. Although born in North Korea during the period of Japanese occupation and raised in a family that "had nothing to do with Christianity," Miss Kim's association followed an internal struggle about "the purpose of life" at age sixteen. Resolving, finally to "go to a church and see what they offer," her involvement quickly progressed to regular attendance, private prayers, vigils, and later, a number of visionary experiences.[1]

Academic study was a second formative influence. A graduate of government-run (i.e., Japanese-run) high school and teacher training school in Seoul, she attended Kwansei Gakuin University in Japan and gained admission to the Methodist seminary there. On graduating, she taught at a women's Bible college in northern Korea and, after World War II, at Ewha University in Seoul where she was professor of New Testament and Comparative Religions. According to a church source, she at that time "was a noted woman intellectual in Korean society."[2] She did postgraduate work at Emmanuel College at the University of Toronto on a scholarship from the United Church of Canada from 1948 to 1951 and spent six months afterwards attending international Christian conferences in Germany and Switzerland.

Conversion

Miss Kim first met the Unification Church in late 1954. According to one source, she was dispatched by the president of Ewha University to investigate the teachings of the new group and bring back the students and several faculty who had become involved.[3] Miss Kim's own account is somewhat different:

> A friend of mine who was not very close to me, a lady, came to me and said, "I found a small group in town . . . in which a young man, who has received a special revelation in the past twenty years from God, is now revealing, unfolding his revelation, a new truth. According to this new truth, God has already started a new dispensation on earth, and the New Testament Age is now over. Because of this new dispensation, God is outpouring His spirit to people on earth. You must come and listen to this man's revelation, and see if this is truth from God or not."[4]

Whichever account is a closer approximation of events (both may be true), the more important question is why Miss Kim agreed to go, especially since returning from Europe, she had suffered from acute indigestion and was confined to her bed. The basic reason for her interest, according to the sources available, related to a pervasive contradiction in her experience. As she put it, "My private prayer or my inner spiritual life and my academic study could not be reconciled." This contradiction might have remained dormant or at least manageable had not her physical affliction brought it to the surface. She stated:

> Physically, I was just skin and bones. I didn't eat normal food for a long time. Spiritually, I wasn't ready to die. I had to accomplish something; I did not know what it was. My mission was not fulfilled.[5]

Resolved to go "even if I died on the street," Miss Kim met Rev. Moon at a private residence in Seoul on December 27, 1954, and at 2:00 p.m. began hearing the new message or "Principle" in lecture form from Mr. Hyo Won Eu. The lecture cycle lasted three days, and though skeptical of certain Bible interpretations, she accepted the teaching based on three factors: affinities between the lecture on "Creation" and "the writings of Swedenborg which interested me very much,"[6] members' testimonies which she deemed authentic, and her own "quite unexpected" experience:

> The third morning when I got up, my diarrhea stopped, my kidney was cleared up, my swelling gone and I felt so light inside . . . when you have diarrhea day after day, you feel so dull. Now I felt so light inside and had a real appetite. I ate fish, pork and spicy pickle . . . Digestion was one hundred percent good! I couldn't understand it. So I asked the leader, "I didn't even ask for healing. How did this happen to me?" He smiled and said, "It is not strange at all . . . You stay here and see what kind of things happen in this group."[7]

Mission

Miss Kim did stay and remained a full four years at Seoul headquarters from the day she accepted the Principle. During those four years before departing as the first Unification Church missionary to America, she took an active role in church organization, teaching and witnessing. Although expelled from her post at Ewha along with four other faculty members and thirteen students (all asked to choose between the university and church), she took a part-time instructorship at lesser known Konkuk University in Seoul and a full-time position as stenographer in the chaplain's office at the United States Eighth Army base, where she recruited two Korean aides de camp.[8] Equally important was her translation of notes from Mr. Eu's lectures into English, assisted by a Pastor McCabe from the

Australian Apostolic Mission who, when asked, suggested she use the title "The Divine Principle" for her book.[9] Miss Kim's 1956 text was the first of continuous efforts on her part to develop an adequate English translation. In this sense, her conversion was coupled with a call to the West. As she put it,

> As soon as I discovered the universal value of the Divine Principles and the heavenly dispensation, I began to be concerned with the people of the Western world with whom I had established a cultural bond. Not only did I feel this, but in the rest of the membership there was no one else at that time who could undertake the job of bringing the Principle to the West.[10]

The Mission to Oregon

Miss Kim was a Unification Church missionary in Oregon from January 4, 1959 until late November, 1960. The pattern of mission and church life that emerged during these two years was influential on later developments. For this reason, it is worthwhile to consider Miss Kim's initiatives in outreach and organization.

Outreach

Miss Kim had relative autonomy in developing the Oregon mission. Rev. Moon, as she noted, had given her "no guidance regarding the work I had to do: what was to be done, how it should be done, where to start. He was only happy to see the realization of the Western mission."[11] While this may have been an advantage, she also faced a number of disadvantages. The first of these was her visa status. Having come to the University of Oregon in Eugene as a student (the only other way out of Korea was as a diplomat), the demands of full-time course work necessary to maintain her legal status exerted constant pressure. A second obstacle was financial. Although the Korean church

collected enough money to cover her travel expenses, Miss Kim
was on her own after that. A third disadvantage was cultural.
This problem was less a matter of Miss Kim's adaptability to
American life than it was the lack of an adequate English edition
of the Principle text. Balanced against these disadvantages were
Miss Kim's initiatives in outreach. Although varied, these
initiatives followed a two step sequence: the singling out of
target populations and the development of methods or strategies
to reach those populations.

Initially fired with hopes of quickly reaching "church people"
and "outstanding individuals with leadership potential," Miss
Kim soon modified these aspirations. Rather than mainline
churches, she began to seek out pentecostal prayer groups and
new age spiritual fellowships that were more open to new truth.
Rather than with leaders, her contacts were with lay people who
were more likely to respond.

Methods and strategies utilized by Miss Kim varied
according to the target population. Early on, she "decided to
write an article and submit it to a number of Christian
magazines." Entitled, "The Cross Is Not Enough," she submitted
it to seventy selected magazines from the Christian Yearbook.
The result was thirty-six standard rejections, six rejections on the
basis of length, and nine rejections on the basis of theological
disagreement.[12]

With a modification in target population, Miss Kim similarly
modified her method from an impersonal mass appeal to a more
personalized approach. Here, her Korean identity was an asset
not only in initiating conversations but also in securing
invitations to lecture before groups. These were occasions of
personal testimony and of sharing mimeographed chapters from
her retranslation (in progress) of the Principle. Traveling via
Greyhound, Miss Kim cultivated a circuit of contacts extending
from Eugene to Portland, Canby, Salem, Corvallis, and
Lebanon. As a result of her efforts, a number of people were
interested to learn more. This necessitated a move beyond
outreach.

Organization

Miss Kim called the first group meeting for those who had studied the Principle on February 13, 1960. From that point, regular meetings were held in the Eugene, Oregon Women's Club where Miss Kim stayed and at the homes of contacts. Although a dozen or so regularly attended, the most promising were three neighbors — Doris Walder Anteloch, Pauline Phillips Sherman, and Patty Pumphrey — from Oakhill, a semi-rural settlement several miles east of Eugene. Miss Kim initially met Doris through a Methodist prayer group, and Doris introduced her to Pauline and Patty. This last contact was fortuitous in that Patty and her husband, Galen, asked Miss Kim, who "was running out of money and could no longer afford to live in Eugene,"[13] to move into a vacant house on their property.

Miss Kim moved to Oakhill on May 14, 1960. Until coming to the San Francisco Bay Area in November, this was her base of operations. The previous March, having "established a spiritual foothold," she left school "to devote . . . full time to the work." The move to Oakhill altered the character of that work. Rather than traveling to other cities, Miss Kim devoted her time during her stay at Oakhill "to raising those who were there, showing them how to lead meetings and living in day to day application of the Principle."[14] Raising "members" also accentuated the need for an adequate text and organizational identity.

Much of Miss Kim's first year in Oregon was spent retranslating the Principle from her earlier effort in Korea. Beginning work in April, 1959, she finished translating the first six chapters (Part I) in June and the second six chapters (Part II) on August 15th.[15] On September 16, 1959, she finished typing the translation. The following March, she typed the manuscript on stencils. At Oakhill, on an IBM executive typewriter rented for one month beginning July 15, 1960, she "began typing the manuscript of the first edition of the Principle in book form." Possibly more than any other factor this task solidified the

Oakhill community. If Miss Kim "literally worked 16 hours a day" justifying right hand margins on the typewriter, "everyone else was kept busy with proofreading." When the time came for offset printing, George Norton, a friend of Galen Pumphrey who had moved into the Oakhill "center" on July 11th, offered his savings of $1,200 to finance the project. The others, according to Miss Kim, "also brought sacrificial contributions."[16]

Along with the Principle text, the emerging consciousness of belonging to an organization also solidified the Oakhill community. Due to the proximity of members, there were more opportunities for meetings and as Miss Kim noted, "We began using a blackboard, took the first photographs of the group, and George Norton taped our meeting for the first time." In mid-June, 1960, the group decided to call its organization the Spiritual Association for the Unification of Christianity.

The need for organizational identity was also accentuated by the presence of another Unification Church missionary from Korea. David S.C. Kim, a founding member of HSA-UWC in 1954, had arrived on September 18, 1959 to attend Western Conservative Baptist Seminary in Portland, Oregon. Like Miss Kim, he began witnessing and had gathered several students. The first joint meeting between the two groups took place in Lebanon, Oregon in July, 1960. A larger joint meeting of twenty persons was held there on September 4th.

Flight to San Francisco

Whether or not Miss Kim's and David Kim's groups could have joined forces following the September 4th joint meeting, they were not given the chance as on the 11th, according to Miss Kim's *Memoirs*, "Doris and Pauline left Oakhill." The reasons for their departure were complex and controversial. According to Miss Kim, "Their husbands . . . were persecuting them. Finally, they could bear it no longer and left without a definite destination." On the other hand, both husbands subsequently sought and gained uncontested divorces on the grounds of "cruel and inhuman treatment."[17] In any case, Miss Kim received a letter from Doris and Pauline on September 15th. They had gone to Fresno, California first. On the 30th, they moved into a hotel in San Francisco.

By the end of the year, Miss Kim and the remainder of her Oakhill group (George Norton, Galen and Patty Pumphrey) had relocated to San Francisco. There were three major reasons for the move. Most obvious was the Oakhill incident which made witnessing in the area extremely difficult. Previously, Miss Kim had been ostracized from Eugene by a disaffected contact who had reported her to the FBI as a communist.[18] As a result of the current scandal, prospects in the area were not only extremely bleak but local hostility was running high. Both husbands reportedly "harassed" the group, mainly by target shooting in the field across from Miss Kim's house.[19]

A second and, perhaps, less immediately obvious reason for leaving the area was the presence of David Kim. Although Miss Kim had been elected president and David Kim vice-president at the September joint meeting,[20] differing ideas over financial responsibilities, witnessing, and even the name of the organization were apparent and a potential source of distraction. A final reason for relocation was the perceived limitation of the Northwest area, itself. Although the printed pages for their new text had arrived by early November, the group could not find a suitable bindery in the area. In Miss Kim's words,

> Eugene was a small, conservative city, where I went not by choice, but to follow my scholarship. Next I went to Oakhill, which was only a small settlement in the countryside. There I spent time raising those who had accepted and deepening their understanding of the Principle, as well as teaching the Principle in Lebanon, Salem, Albany, and Portland. I reached out quite widely, considering that I was only one person. I found Oregon quite provincial on the whole, though, and was not reluctant to leave. I yearned to launch my work in

a cosmopolitan city. I now had a textbook for wider
work. Doris and Pauline, who had left sometime
earlier, ended up in San Francisco. It seemed like this
was where Father was leading me.[21]

NOTES

1. Young Oon Kim, "Testimony given at Sacramento, California, August 24 1963," unpublished manuscript.

2. Kwang Yol Yoo, "A History of the Unification Church from the Early Days," *New Hope News*, January 6 1976.

3. Yoo, ibid.

4. Kim, "Testimony."

5. Kim, "Testimony."

6. Young Oon Kim, *Memoirs*, unpublished manuscript, 1954-60.

7. Kim, "Testimony."

8. One of these was Col. Bo Hi Pak, later Rev. Moon's public translator in America.

9. David S.C. Kim, "The Establishment of H.S.A. (Holy Spirit Association) and my Role as one of the Original Participants, *United Temple Bulletin*, May 1970. While on a missionary trip to England in 1955, David Kim spoke before the Apostolic Church International Convention. He stressed the responsibilities of the existing churches "to protect" the Unification movement by sending representatives to study the new message and help. In June 1956, the Apostolic Church despatched McCabe from the Australian mission. Although he assisted Miss Kim in her English translation of The Principle, David Kim reported, "Because of doctrinal differences, the original purpose of helping our movement by foreign missions was not fulfilled."

10. Kim, *Memoirs,* 1954-60.

11. Kim, *Memoirs,* 1954-60.

12. Kim, *Memoirs*, February 1960.

13. Kim, *Memoirs*, April 1960.

14. Kim, *Memoirs*, September 1960.

15. Kim, *Memoirs,* June and August 1960. It is important to note that Miss Kim's translation and chapter divisions were her own and authoritative within her group. Other Unification Church missionaries, including David S.C. Kim and Bo Hi Pak, wrote their own versions of the Principle which were authoritative within their groups.

16. Kim, *Memoirs*, August 1960.

17. Kim, *Memoirs*, Sept. 1960; John Lofland, "The World Savers: A Field Study of Cult Processes," (Ph.D. dissertation, University of California, 1964), 124.

18. Kim, *Memoirs*, March 1960.

19. John Lofland, *Doomsday Cult: A Study of Conversion, Proselytization, and Maintenance of Faith*, enlarged edition (New York: Irvington Publishers, 1977), 247.

20. "Spiritual Association for the Unification of Christianity," *Monthly Newsletter*, December 13, 1960.

21. Kim, *Memoirs*, November 1960.

CHAPTER TWO

TO THE BAY AREA: 1960-63

The Community—Visa Problems—From Community to Corporation—Improving the Text—Friends and Foes—Spreading the Word—Bay Area and Beyond—The Newsletter—Circuit Rider—Training Session Crisis—Success

The story of the Unification Church and its beginnings in the San Francisco Bay Area is not that of a single missionary venturing thousands of miles from her home. It is rather the story of a community of believers transplanting themselves from rural Oregon several hundreds of miles down the coast to the urban environment of the Bay Area. The nature of this community, its struggle to survive, and its attempt to spread its message is the content of this story.

The Community

When Miss Kim arrived in the San Francisco Bay Area on November 21, 1960, Doris and Pauline already had been there for more than a month. George Norton had driven her down from Oakhill. Galen and Patty Pumphrey arrived two weeks later. These six people were the beginning of the Unification Church in the Bay Area. All had severed ties irrevocably with the Northwest. Moreover, unlike in Oakhill where each had maintained separate households, in the Bay Area, they found a seven room flat at 410 Cole Street, San Francisco, and moved in together. Miss Kim noted:

> Our community life really began at this time, in San Francisco. We had decided not to call our group or building a church. . .and referred to the Cole Street house as our Center.[1]

To support themselves, Doris and Pauline acquired jobs as waitresses. George Norton became an orderly in a local hospital, and Galen secured a job as a postman. In terms of secular credentials, the group did not appear overly promising. Only Miss Kim had a college degree. George and Galen had both been to college but dropped out. Doris and Patty had not ventured beyond high school, and Pauline had completed only rural elementary school. At the same time, the group, for all its worldly limitations, was 'confident of its call'. They believed that God, not they, had initiated the new dispensation and had called them to the harvest. They all, like Miss Kim, simply had been 'ready'.

The original community, plus the few associates and new members it was able to gain, stayed together for eighteen months until dispersing to various cities throughout the Bay Area in July, 1962. Its basic task during this period was survival. Although the group had demonstrated considerable solidarity and commitment in migrating south from Oakhill, the challenge to maintain that solidarity and commitment amid an impersonal and sometimes hostile urban environment was considerable. The problems which the community faced were to test it severely.

Visa problems

A continuing source of concern to the community and one that threatened Miss Kim directly were her visa problems. As a student at the University of Oregon, she had had no problems, but after dropping out to devote her energies full time to the mission, Miss Kim was constantly threatened. She faced four separate crises before finally winning an immigrant visa in October, 1963.

The first crisis occurred shortly after arriving in San Francisco. Previously, while in Oregon, Miss Kim had traveled there to obtain an extension of her passport from the Korean consulate. But in late November, 1960, her visa was about to expire again. Therefore, after depositing the Principle at the Trade Bindery and securing a place of residence, Miss Kim's first priority was to apply for an extension of her visa at the Immigration Office. However, this time she was refused.

If Miss Kim were forced to leave the country at this early stage, the consequences would have been grave and possibly fatal for the community. Nonetheless, as her visa had absolutely expired, she went to Japan Airlines and bought a ticket to Korea. A telegram from Rev. Moon arrived on December 11, 1960 which stated, "By all means, you must stay."[2] George and Galen wrote back explaining that there was no way for her to stay.

On December 20th, several of the group visited George White, a lawyer, to see about getting a copyright for the Principle text. Miss Kim happened to mention her visa situation, and he declared that the business of distributing one's book was valid reason for an extension. With instructions to go with her sponsor to the Immigration Office, Miss Kim found her visa extended, "most unexpectedly." She wrote:

> When there appeared to be no way in the world to
> prolong my stay in America, Mr. White appeared on
> the scene and suddenly everything was solved. I
> canceled my flight reservation and lost $20.[3]

In March, 1961, the three month extension Miss Kim won in December was ready to expire again. By this time, though, she had met Dr. John W. Hopkins, President of Williams College in Berkeley.[4] He had arranged to have Miss Kim give several lectures in conjunction with the "School of Metaphysical Inquiry" there, and on hearing of her visa situation, wrote a letter to the Immigration Office explaining that Miss Kim was lecturing at his school and couldn't leave. In this way, the second crisis was averted, and Miss Kim's visa was extended until July 31, 1961.

Miss Kim was pressured by the same problem in July but solved it in a markedly different way; on the 10th, she was ordained at the Universal Church of the Master. As she put it,

> Dr. Hopkins had explained the advantages of ordination in forming a religious organization in America. I had never intended to be ordained, even though I had been offered the opportunity to become a Methodist minister in Korea and was fully qualified . . . I wanted to be, rather, a dedicated layman. It was now necessary, however, for our group to be legally recognized.[5]

Dr. Hopkins knew the Archers, who were ministers in the Universal Church of the Master, and requested that Miss Kim be ordained. They, in turn, contacted Dr. Fitzgerald, President of the church. Out of respect for Dr. Hopkins, he agreed to consider Miss Kim. After prayer, the issue was resolved to the satisfaction of Rev. Archer, and Miss Kim was ordained. Her visa was thereby extended until the following March.

Because her stay in America involved the constant strain of securing temporary visas, Miss Kim decided in December, 1961 to investigate procuring a permanent visa. She consulted Drs. Hopkins and Fitzgerald in January and went to the Immigration Office with her lawyer to inquire what was necessary for a permanent visa application. Essentials included academic records, ordination papers, and the charter of the corporation for which she was ministering.

A year passed, and Miss Kim received no word on her application. Finally, in April, 1963, she began investigating only to find out that the Office had lost track of her application. Unfortunately, Miss Kim's inquiry served to remind them, and they contacted her lawyer to whom they had sent a notice the previous year declaring that Miss Kim's permanent visa was denied. Her lawyer, then, contacted Miss Kim and told her that he had put the notice from the Immigration Office in his drawer a year previously, but he too had completely forgotten about it!

Now, however, the matter was urgent. Miss Kim visited the Immigration Office and was given thirty days to either reapply or leave the country. Though later granted an additional grace period beyond the thirty days, Miss Kim was in a difficult situation. She knew that those applying whose occupation was attached to a corporation would have had to have worked for that corporation for at least a year, Miss Kim understood that she would not be eligible until September. Hence, there was the possibility of her having to leave the country before becoming eligible.

Miss Kim's status might have resulted in deportation had she not suffered a sudden appendicitis attack in June. As a result, she was able to secure a letter from her physician to the Immigration Office explaining that she would be under his care for at least three months. In this way, Miss Kim was able to remain in the country until her eligibility was assured. She wrote:

> My visa petition had lain dormant for a year through most unusual circumstances, having been simultaneously forgotten by the Immigration Office and by my attorney. Now, at the last moment, there seemed to be no way whatsoever to avoid rejection. However, I was granted another stroke of Divine Providence. Though my appendix suffered, the victory was won, in God's ineffable way.[6]

Late in August, Miss Kim was granted an interview at the Immigration Office, and on October 21st, she received her immigrant visa, dated October 9, 1963.

From Community to Corporation

Along with the need to stabilize her own status in the country, Miss Kim recognized the need to incorporate the group. Although she consulted Mr. White about this matter in January, 1961, it wasn't until the following August that she pursued the issue seriously, and then largely for visa purposes. It also became clear that for tax exemption purposes and legal protection it was necessary for the group to be recognized by the government and receive legal status as a religion.

In order to prepare the necessary papers, Miss Kim obtained a legal book about incorporation which she studied thoroughly. She then drafted Articles of Incorporation. To be consistent with the Korean church, she changed the name of the group to the "Holy Spirit Association for the Unification of World Christianity." Miss Kim signed the paper of incorporation at her lawyer's office, and on September 18, 1961, the Articles of Incorporation were filed by the state of California.

Incorporation necessitated annual meetings for the election of officers and the formulation of bylaws. Beyond this, the process conferred a sense of stability and substance to the group. Amended in 1963, her California corporation became and still is the legal basis of HSA-UWC in America. Original signers of this document were Young Oon Kim, Doris Walder, Galen Pumphrey, George Norton, and William Delaney.

Improving the Text

Closely related to Miss Kim's and the group's efforts to attain secure standing were continual efforts to produce an adequate printed text of the Principle. This, of course, had been a persistent concern of Miss Kim since her first translation of the lectures into English. In Oregon, she spent countless hours revising the English translation. The book underwent three editions during her stay in the Bay Area.

Having arrived in the San Francisco Bay Area with the printed and collated pages of *The Divine Principles*, Miss Kim's first stop was the Trade Bindery to inquire about getting the books bound. Leaving three copies to be bound as samples, the group began checking page sequences of the collated books, a job which took three days. After deciding to go ahead with the binding, Miss Kim visited the Internal Revenue Service to see about getting a permit to sell the book and a lawyer, George White, about getting a copyright. On December 31, 1960, the cloth covers arrived at the bindery, and on January 6, 1961, members brought home 100 bound copies of the first edition.

Although it was a breakthrough, the first edition contained many errors, both grammatical and typographical. As people noticed these, Miss Kim spent endless hours going through the nearly 500 copies, "pasting correction slips over large errors and rectifying smaller ones by hand." In July, 1961, after many weeks of "polishing the English," Miss Kim began typing the second edition with editorial help from one of George Norton's acquaintances.[7]

The community purchased a printing machine in November, and they decided to print the second edition themselves. Galen Pumphrey's bedroom became the first Unification Church print shop in America, and by January, he and George Norton had learned how to operate the press. During this time, Miss Kim continued typing and proofreading the new edition. On January 1, 1962, they began to print.

Although far from professional, George and Galen did a credible job, and starting February 5th, everyone was at work gathering and folding the pages they had printed. This job continued for six days, and on February 11th they took 500 copies to the Trade Bindery. Three days later they received back 110 copies and in March, 1962, the remainder of the second edition.

While the second edition was far better than the first, by October, 1962, Miss Kim had begun making revisions and typing out the manuscript for the third edition. In part, this new effort came at the urging of Gordon Ross, a new member and former Woodrow Wilson scholar in linguistics at the University of California at Berkeley. He pointed out deficiencies in the text that had hindered his study and which if not amended would in his view lead scholars to dismiss it.

This time, Miss Kim was anxious to produce an authoritative version. She finished typing the manuscript on December 1, 1962, and proofreading began two days later with Gordon Ross and John Lofland, a doctoral student in Sociology at the University of California who was studying the group. They finished on December 5th. A second proofreading began on the 9th and finished on the 11th.

Consistent with the desire to produce an authoritative edition, the group decided to use a professional printer. Miss Kim inquired about rates in Japan and Hong Kong. Although the rates were cheaper, shipping costs nullified any advantages, and the job was given to Kingsport Press. The galley proofs arrived in May, and on October 8, 1963, 1,625 copies of the third edition arrived from. This edition was authoritative in Miss Kim's group for the next four years.

Friends and Foes

While visas, incorporation papers, and successive texts helped root the transplanted community in its new environment and foster survival, another important factor was the community's interaction with outsiders. Whether they were friends or foes was not so important as the fact that they helped bridge the gap between community aspirations and an otherwise impersonal, unresponsive social environment. Although few contacts joined the community, they helped energize it. Basically, these significant others fell into five categories: the occult milieu, church people, Korean visitors, legal authorities, and academics.

The occult milieu

Among the most important friends of the Unification Church movement during this period in the Bay Area were the loose associations of those involved in what has been termed the occult milieu. Describing themselves, according to one account, as "students of metaphysics . . . seeking enlightenment in the higher spiritual realms," this subculture included a broad crosssection of American people, though with a preponderance of middle-aged and older women.[8]

Miss Kim already had been exposed to this subculture in her early study of Swedenborg and in Oregon where she had contacted the Spiritual Frontiers Fellowship. Besides seekers eager for the newest message, the occult milieu also included spiritualists and mediums ready with prophecy or affirming messages from the spiritual world. In the Bay Area when the Unification movement was largely impotent, their messages were immensely consoling and vital for the survival of the community. Four of these contacts are noteworthy.

Rev. Clyde Dibble. Assistant minister and himself a medium at Golden Gate Spiritualist Church in San Francisco, Rev. Dibble met the community shortly after their arrival. Not only did he help Galen get a job at the post office but in late January, 1961, he visited the center. Sitting in a semicircle, the group asked questions about spiritual phenomena. Miss Kim recalled:

> He kept glancing over at me, and finally, as if he could hold back no longer, said, "I see such great light around you!" He answered a few more questions and then, closing his eyes, rose to his feet. It was apparent to all of us that he was in a trance. He bowed deeply to me three times and said, "It is Lao-tsu." Then he bowed twice more and said, "It is White Cloud, an Indian Chief." White Cloud and Lao-tsu both brought messages which promised great blessings to our group and spoke of the way our movement would flourish and grow in the future.[9]

Dr John W Hopkins. President of Williams College in Berkeley and himself an occult enthusiast, Dr. Hopkins offered Miss Kim not a dramatic prophecy but a chance to speak. The following announcement from his school's monthly flyer of March, 1961, well illustrates the openness of the occult milieu to new revelations:

> Wednesday, March 15, at 8:00 p.m., a lecture by Young Oon Kim, B.A., B.Th., B.D., of Korea on: *The Divine Principles.* Miss Kim is a teacher of the New Age, giving principles from Divine revelation as taught and verified by her from a Master teacher (whom she will reveal in her lecture). She will give a history of her Master teacher and show his direct revelations pertaining to the end of this civilization or the last days of it and the ushering in its place of the New Age . . . Miss Kim shows further, as is explained also by her book, "The Divine Principles," how her teacher reveals the Divine schedule of Cosmic restoration including fallen mankind . . . The New Age will bring one world, one religion, one language, and other unities as well as perfect harmony of spirit and of body.[10]

Rev. Louis Lusardi and Rev. Julian Levy. Two San Francisco mediums contacted by Patty Pumphrey, the Reverends Lusardi and Levy, unlike others, heard the Principle and affiliated themselves with the community as outside members.[11] Although both had disassociated themselves from active involvement by mid-1963, their presence was not without significance. For example, when one member wanted to move out, the two had simultaneous visions:

> Rev. Levy saw a field of wheat so heavy with grain that the tops of the plants were bent over. Then he saw a small lamb creeping in the field crying out, "I'm so hungry! Oh, I'm so hungry!" The lamb only looked at the ground. It never lifted up its head to see the ripe

grain. If it had only looked up, it would have had
plenty to eat.

Rev. Lusardi saw a tired traveler in the burning
desert doggedly following a small candle through the
night. The candle led to the edge of a land that was
filled with bright sunlight where there was a white
castle. As soon as the traveler reached the border into
that land the light of the candle disappeared. The
traveler looked around for the candle and reentered the
desert to find it. Once again the candle led him to the
light, and once again the traveler left the bright land to
find the candle.[12]

An interesting "New Age" variation on the pseudepigrapha
of Jewish apocalyptic writings was the lengthy text of "Spiritual
Communication with the Apostle Paul: Given Through the
Clairaudient Mediumship of Rev. Louis Lusardi, May 20-May
21, 1962." Purported to be the four hour dictation of the Apostle
Paul to Rev. Lusardi while the latter was on night shift at a local
hotel, the manuscript described the relationship of Jesus to the
New Age.

Emilia Rathbun. Wife of a retired Stanford University
professor, Mrs. Emilia L. Rathbun "received" that "she was the
leader of the New Age in America and that her mission was to
gather 1000 American women." Through Pauline, Miss Kim met
Mrs. Rathbun in late December, 1962, and offered her
assessment:

> She [Emilia] was a charming, gracious woman. She
> was articulate and refined, but her work lacked a clear
> message and purpose. I hoped she would redefine her
> mission in light of the Principle and follow.[13]

Although Mrs. Rathbun never did follow (nor, presumably, find
her 1000 women), the kind of exuberance and hope such
encounters engendered were well expressed in Pauline's later
report:

> Miss Kim and I went to Palo Alto on the 18th of
> December and had a meeting with Mr. and Mrs.
> Rathbun and three other ladies. They were very much
> moved by Miss Kim's life story and the message. They
> bought books and wanted to start a study group in the
> home of Mrs. Rathbun, who had received parts of the
> Principle . . . Later she took Miss Kim in her arms and
> cried and said, "My sister, my sister!" We were all so
> happy. We know there are many people just waiting for
> us to bring the message to them. We have to be like a
> detective for God and find them quickly.[14]

Christian Churches

Christian churches and church people were, in a very real
sense, the first target group of Miss Kim's community and the
intended recipients of the new message. That the churches were,
in fact, more 'foe' than 'friend' did less to discourage the
community than it did to convince them that their message was
authentic. As Miss Kim wrote in a sermon entitled, "Suffering
Is a Privilege,"

> When we are insulted and rejected by the Christians
> because of our message, we know exactly how Jesus
> felt when he was insulted and rejected by the Jewish
> people. When we are rejected, mocked, and persecuted
> because of the Divine Principles we teach, we are
> privileged to experience a small percentage of the
> thorny path our Leader has gone through.[15]

Although no church leaders, ministers, or educators
converted, the earliest Unification Church community in the San
Francisco Bay Area (unlike others that followed) emphasized
church visitation. Bay Area churches in the early 1960s reflected
conservative and liberal traditions as well as newly emergent
charismatic and ecumenical trends. Miss Kim's group met
representatives from each of these four groupings.

Conservative. A Baptist minister in whose church members had 'witnessed' several times, Dr. Curtis Nims was a representative of orthodox, conservative, evangelical Christianity. In February, 1962, he sent one of his parishioners to investigate the group. Shortly afterwards, Miss Kim and the group received a letter from Dr. Nims excoriating them and denouncing the teaching. Although he later bought the Principle book, Miss Kim retained the check he gave in payment on which he had written it was a "cult" book and a "spurious approach to Christianity."[16] On February 18, 1962, Dr Nim's declared Miss Kim a heretic from his pulpit.

Liberal. Bishop of the Episcopal Diocese of California and proprietor of Grace Cathedral in San Francisco, James A. Pike encountered the Unification Church as a result of handbills passed out by members on the steps of his cathedral. This activity provoked one of his priests who ran out and grabbed the handbills. Enraged, the priest forbade members to engage in that again and threatened to take action if they disobeyed.

To forestall this kind of occurrence, Miss Kim visited Bishop Pike the day after the incident. This visit was significant to the community in two ways: first, in that Miss Kim could gain access to an important church official; and second, in that she could see the stranglehold organizational bureaucracy had on the church. Not only did Bishop Pike seem undisturbed that they had been passing out handbills near his cathedral but, according to Miss Kim, "He said that he envied me because I was able to devote my life to religious work."[17]

Charismatic renewal. Rector of an Episcopal parish in Corte Madera which was attracting parishioners from all over the Bay Area due to its tongues-speaking services, Rev. Tod Ewald was a participant in the newly emergent charismatic revival. Pauline Phillips had found out about the church and in January, 1963, Miss Kim attended a prayer meeting. A week later, she attended again, shared some spiritual experiences, and met Rev. Ewald. Invited to speak at the next pentecostal meeting, she and Gordon Ross offered their testimonies. While the response of the

audience was encouraging, even more propitious was Rev.
Ewald's reaction. Miss Kim wrote:

> After the meeting Rev. Ewald asked to see us in his
> office. There he knelt and asked us to place our hands
> on his head and bless him. He felt that we were much
> richer in spirit than himself.[18]

Although Rev. Ewald later drew the ire of the church hierarchy
his witness was inspiring to the fledgling community.

Ecumenism. Along with the charismatic revival, another
important development among Bay Area churches in the early
1960s was the ecumenical movement. It was particularly strong
in Berkeley where in 1962 four Protestant seminaries (Baptist,
Episcopalian, Lutheran, and Presbyterian) incorporated the
Graduate Theological Union as a common instrument for their
doctoral programs. At the same time, churches surrounding the
University of California were working together and formed the
University Church Council as an outreach to the campus.

Gordon Ross, a former seminarian at Pacific Lutheran
Theological Seminary and active participant on the University
Church Council, had many contacts among ecumenically minded
churches. Although none of his contacts accepted the Principles,
the hostility with which many of them rejected the new message
only affirmed his appreciation of its potency. Telling of an
encounter with one minister on the University Church Council,
he wrote:

> In the course of conversation, he called me neurotic,
> psychotic, a termite in the Christian Church and told
> me to stay away from Presbyterians. I told him that I
> had a job to do, that I had to follow my conscience,
> and he walked away . . . my heart was broken at this
> reception, not for my sake, but for his.[19]

Pauline Phillips, who often accompanied Gordon, was less
conciliatory:

> The Church is our worst enemy. Ministers and teachers
> do not want to lose their hold over the people. They are
> very jealous-natured people.[20]

Korean visitors

The most important Korean visitor scheduled to visit the San Francisco Bay Area community was Rev. Moon, who planned to come to America in the spring of 1961. Miss Kim obtained a visa, and the group purchased a camper for travels following his expected arrival in late May. However, these plans were jarred by the Korean military coup of May 16, 1961 and subsequent prohibitions on foreign travel. Waiting hopefully into the late summer, the group finally received word that Rev. Moon had decided not to come.

While this news was disappointing, the community still had significant contacts with two Korean visitors, one of whom was a force behind the military junta which had prevented Rev. Moon's travel.

Jong Pil Kim. Chairman of the newly emerged Supreme Council for National Reconstruction (SCNR) in Korea, Jong Pil Kim journeyed to the United States in November, 1961, for talks with American leaders and a meeting with President John Kennedy. After the talks, he spent two days in San Francisco before returning to Korea. During his stay in the Bay Area, Miss Kim received a call from a Colonel Han, a church member and one of Jong Pil Kim's aides and interpreters. He had arranged for Miss Kim and five American members not only to attend a reception but also to have an audience with the chairman.

At the reception, members met another aide who had recently joined the church, and in the private audience Miss Kim spoke of her work in America. In addition, each American member gave a brief testimony of their experiences with the church. While the meeting was relatively routine, its significance was enormous for a community which was struggling with obscurity and rejection.

Bo Hi Pak. Military Attache at the Korean Embassy in Washington and later Rev. Moon's chief public translator in America, Colonel Bo Hi Pak first visited the San Francisco Bay Area with his wife en route to his post in Washington. A dedicated member since being led to the movement in 1957 by Miss Kim, Col. Pak began missionary activities in Washington, D.C. within the context of his diplomatic career much in the same way as Miss Kim had done as a student. He spoke widely in churches, established a Bible study group, and by early 1963, had set up a karate institute with his cousin, Jhoon Rhee. [21]

Col. Pak was also helpful in securing a loan to finance the third edition of the Principle book. However, in March, 1963, Miss Kim received disturbing news that Col. Pak had incorporated a separate association in Arlington, Virginia. On embassy business to the Bay Area in August of that year, the situation was not ameliorated by Col. Pak's proposal to write "another book on the Principle." [22] Although Miss Kim, herself, later relocated in Washington, D.C., it was clear in 1963 that if not factionalized, there was at least competition within missionary ranks.

Civil authorities

Apart from visa problems and the process of incorporation, the Bay Area community of 1960 to 1963 had surprisingly little contact with civil authorities. This was especially remarkable in that the community was highly committed, communal and conversion-orientated. The only real exception to this situation was a continuing struggle with the San Francisco Department of Building Inspection in May and June, 1962.

In January of that year, the group signed a contract to purchase a large, three story building at 1309 Masonic Avenue, San Francisco. The group was tired of throwing away their money each month on rent, and as the building had three separate flats, it was conceived of as a place for Rev. Moon and possible training site for future missionaries. The group came up with the necessary $2000 downpayment and in March, 1962, moved in.

The community engaged in an extensive renovation effort for the next two months. Walls were steamed in preparation for painting, floors were sanded, and the accumulated grime of decades removed. By May, the building was in shape, and Galen Pumphrey worked for several days to make a large, four-by-five foot signboard which read:

THE DIVINE PRINCIPLE
CENTER
Proclaiming God's New Revelation
Lectures Daily 2 p.m. & 8 p.m.
Meetings Tues. and Fri. 7:30 p.m.
1309 Masonic Ave. MA1-6609[23]

Hung from the second floor window, the sign was large enough for both pedestrians and traffic to see. The local building inspector also noticed it, and two days later issued a warning that to open a public assembly hall fire equipment needed to be installed, fire exits marked, etc.—improvements which would cost $3,000-$4,000. On consulting their lawyer and the ACLU, members found that this was true, and on the following day, the inspector demanded that the sign be taken down and all meetings stopped. This precipitated a serious dilemma for the center that was solved only by the rental of a tiny storefront church at 290 Valencia Street, an area crowded with bars, garages and slum tenements. Their 'church in exile' continued the confrontation with the Department of Inspection for the remainder of May and most of June, 1962.

Still living at the center, the group was informed on June 4, 1962 that the plumbing was inadequate. Having fixed that, they then were required to change the wiring and install fire escapes. The group sensed that someone was instigating these inspections. Indignant, Miss Kim wrote a letter to the Superintendent of the Bureau of Building Inspection:

I confronted him with the unfairness of making our house the target of numerous inspections when there were such flagrant, unnoticed violations elsewhere. We had renovated the entire house so that it was transformed. Why now should there be a siege of inspections when the house had been untouched for years? I informed him that we knew who had directed the Department so exclusively to us. . .

Two days later the inspector came and expressed his apologies . . . we removed the sign from the Valencia street church and resumed meetings at the center on Masonic. However, we didn't put the sign board up again.[24]

Academics

Given the limitations of text and membership, the movement's contact with Bay Area academics was necessarily limited, although not without import. The role of Dr. Hopkins, President of Williams College in Berkeley, in offering Miss Kim the opportunity to speak at his school already has been noted. Although the response of seminary professors was negligible, a number of individuals from the larger academic community contributed to group's development.

Swami Amar Jyoti. A Hindu leader who came to America and spoke in various cities to generate interest in his ashram and future international school in India, Swami Amar Jyoti spent four days at the Unification center while visiting the Bay Area in September 1961. Miss Kim, who had been Professor of Comparative Religions at Ehwa University in Korea, was most interested. During his stay, the Swami lectured on self realization, demonstrated Yoga techniques, and spoke about India while members taught him the Principle. Although neither side converted, they remained friends and Swami Amar Jyoti's future letters were recorded in the group's newsletters.

Guest speakers. Experts in various subjects or disciplines were often invited to the center to speak. This practice was especially pronounced during the summer of 1962 after purchasing the Masonic Avenue house and resolving the conflict with the Department of Inspection. Guests included the superintendent of a large mental hospital, a customs collector, a sociologist, a surgeon, a political analyst from the International Institute, a psychiatrist, and an ex-Rosicrucianist. Most of these guests were Ph.D.'s. Although none converted, their presence and talks helped lend stature to the community.

John Lofland. A Ph.D. student in sociology at the University of California at Berkeley, John Lofland met Doris Walder at a UFO convention and after several preliminary contacts, decided to do his doctoral dissertation on the group. Having obtained permission from Miss Kim to move in, Lofland played a decisive, if puzzling and finally troublesome role in the community's development. As a participant observer from March, 1962, until January, 1963, when he was asked to leave, Lofland represented the movement's first encounter with a 'disinterested' academic investigator. The misunderstandings that accrued in this encounter were heated and difficult. Miss Kim asserted,

> I rather naively thought that he would write a neutral history of our movement. But I saw more and more that he was not genuine and that his view was distorted. His sarcasm became more and more open and his derogatory conception of our work became more obvious. I told him finally, to move out and not come to our meetings.[25]

For his own part, John Lofland later wrote in the methodological appendix to his thesis:

> It seems, in fact, that for eleven months I had un-wittingly and systematically mislead the DP's with the *standard participant observer's* open, permissive, sympathetic stance. While I was trying to appear noncommittal, although very interested, the DP's were

> reading this as existential concern. Lee [i.e., Miss Kim]
> now decided I was unlikely to convert, and so there
> was no longer any justification for my presence.[26]

Whichever interpretation was accurate, there was little question, as Lofland later noted, that "the presence of one who is not quite a member inherently involves some difficulties for all the parties."[27]

"The World Savers: A Field Study of Cult Processes," Lofland's 588-page dissertation, was submitted to and approved by the University of California at Berkeley's department of sociology in June, 1964. In 1966, the thesis was published in abridged form by Prentice-Hall, as *Doomsday Cult: A Study of Conversion, Proselytization, and Maintenance of Faith*. Lofland went on to teach at the University of Michigan; Sonoma State College, California; and the University of California at Davis.

Despite the use of pseudonyms in both of his studies (i.e., Bay City = San Francisco; Miss Lee = Miss Kim; Northwest Town = Eugene), neither the dissertation nor the published work were appreciated or acknowledged by the group. Miss Kim wrote, "By ignoring it completely, we showed our disapproval and could not be held responsible for the content."[28] On the other hand, Lofland's work, especially his theory of conversion, was well received in sociological circles.[29]

Spreading the Word

Beyond survival, Miss Kim's group's purpose in coming to the Bay Area was to spread the message of Divine Principle, to win those who responded, and to send these fellow laborers off to new mission fields. The practicalities of visas, incorporation papers, improvement of the text, and community development were all secondary to the primary task of evangelization. Nonetheless, because the message was new, because the community was inexperienced, and because potential converts were less plentiful than in the late 1960s, spreading the message was difficult.

John Lofland described the "DP's proselytization activities" in terms of "two temporally sequential phases":

> 1. *Strategies of access*. In what ways and under what conditions can missionaries gain access to and the attention of non-believers for the purpose of conversion?
> 2. *Promotion of conversion*. After gaining access, what are the ways in which missionaries can attempt to promote prospects into accepting a world view? [30]

Within each of these phases, Lofland lists several other categories. Classed under "strategies of access" were "*embodied* (face-to-face) and *disembodied* (mediated) communications." Classed under "conversion- promotion tactics" were "the briefing session" and "the study group."[31] Although Lofland's research was limited to eleven months between February, 1962, and January, 1963, his analysis is useful in understanding not only sociological processes of Miss Kim's group but also its historical development.

Strategies of access

Having come to the cosmopolitan Bay Area, Miss Kim's group quickly sought to reach the populace with their message. Lofland noted:

> Now assembled in Bay City (i.e. San Francisco), DP's saw themselves as a saved remnant with a new world before them waiting to be conquered. Hope of imminent success was strong.[32]

The group, however, found that it was one thing to have the message and quite another thing to spread it. During years 1960-63, they experimented with numerous strategies to reach the larger population. Their "disembodied" attempts can be grouped into two divisions: first, public lecture series; and second, handbills, ads, personals, articles, and letters. Almost without exception, these attempts were failures.

The first effort of the group to move the city came in early January, 1961, shortly after their arrival in San Francisco. Galen persuaded Miss Kim to rent a hall and offered to lecture the Principle. With great anticipation, the group rented the Lions Club Hall for a series of four Mondays and placed an ad in the classified section of the San Francisco *Chronicle*:

> A NEW MESSAGE
> Never told before. Reason and
> Purpose of Creation — What God is going
> to do in the next 7 years.
> Lectures Mondays 7:30 p.m. January 9th,
> 16th, 23rd, 30th. No charges, San Francisco
> Lions Club Hall, 772 Clayton Street.

The results were not gratifying. Miss Kim noted, "Despite our preparation and hope, only one man showed up. The lecture Galen had planned was instead an informal chat. We canceled the hall."[33]

The next public talk attempted by the group was Miss Kim's March, 1961, speech at Williams College's School of Metaphysical Inquiry. Given wide notice in the school's March flyer, fifty-two people attended. As a result, it was arranged for Miss Kim to teach a regular class, and the school's April flyer announced her lectures. Unfortunately, this effort repeated the pattern of the Lions Club. John Lofland reported:

> Those interested had . . . apparently heard enough the first time. Not a single person appeared for Lee's [i.e., Kim's] first class, and the rest of them were canceled.[34]

By September, 1961, the group was ready to try again with a public lecture series, although this time utilizing a different medium. As Miss Kim put it,

> We were impatient with the slow expansion of our movement and were looking for ways to make our message known more quickly. We decided to look into radio broadcasting.[35]

After finding the prices or requirements of most stations prohibitive, several members had an interview with Pastor Jim, who had a program on KSAN, a local religious station with a largely black audience. At eighteen dollars for fifteen minutes each Sunday morning from 9:15-9:30, the group contracted to do a series of taped broadcasts for eight Sundays. Miss Kim wrote eleven talks covering all twelve chapters of the Principle, Doris did the reading, and George Norton taped them. Running from late September to the first Sunday in November, 1961, "The Age of Restoration" radio broadcasts were disappointing. John Lofland noted:

> The total result was two phone calls, one from a bed-ridden elderly lady . . . and another from negro minister. Neither appeared at the DP center.[36]

Making the most of their 'exile' to Brother Bob Guajao's storefront church during their dispute with the Building Inspector, the group decided on yet another public lecture series, this time a "Bible Week" to begin Tuesday, June 12, 1962. They had some months before obtained a permit to operate a sound truck, and beginning June 8th, George Norton rode the streets of San Francisco with a repeating thirty-second tape of Doris' voice:

> Ladies and gentlemen, we are proclaiming God's new revelation, the Divine Principle. This message gives the answer to the worldwide turmoil and what will happen

in the earth in the next few years. We have entered,
since 1960, the Golden Age. Come and listen at 290
Valencia nightly at 7:30.[37]

Again, the results were less than spectacular. According to
Lofland,

> On opening night, Tuesday the 12th, twelve DP's and
> sundry hangers-on appeared at the storefront church.
> They far outnumbered the audience: an emaciated
> working-class male who left after an hour; a fortyish
> Filipino male who sat reading a newspaper; a sixtyish
> working-class female who walked out within twenty
> minutes; and three small boys, aged nine or ten, who
> were ushered out because of loud play.[38]

Besides public lecture series, Miss Kim's group
experimented with other mass-oriented appeals, all with limited
success. Before and after the Lions Club episode, the group
printed handbills and distributed them door-to-door and at Union
Square in downtown San Francisco. While the handbills did
contain basic information such as a Post Office box number for
purchasing books and a phone number to call for further study,
John Lofland's comments are instructive:

> Unlike most handbills, this one was long and complex.
> It was typed single-spaced, filling the entire sheet with
> almost fifty lines of text. Unlike the usual handbill style
> of frequent capitalization, not a single word was in
> capitals and no part stood out. It was hardly designed
> to catch even a fleeting interest. It was rather the sort
> of document one had to study; it embodied a
> meticulous, academic approach to the problem of access
> and interest development.[39]

Along with handbills, the group tried conventional ads in the
Saturday religion section of the newspaper, again with limited

success. More promising, at least initially, were the 'personals'. The first of these, Patty Pumphrey's, appeared in the San Francisco *Chronicle*, Sunday, June 24, 1962: "For the key to perfection, call MA 1-6609."

Unlike the conventional ads, this one brought a heavy response. Lofland noted, "People may not have been interested in new revelations, but they were at least intrigued by perfection." Unfortunately, not all callers were serious:

> By the end of the week the ad had more nuisance than access value. There was much phone ringing and much baiting and hanging up.[40]

In September, the group tried again, placing three personals, one per week, in the Sunday *Chronicle*:

> WHY the rapid increase of suicide today? MA 1-6609
> WHY the vast amount of mental illness in San
>   Francisco? MA 1-6609
> WHO can stop moral decay? MA 1-6609

Again, the results were distracting:

> The phone began ringing twenty to thirty times a day. About half offered nothing but the click of a phone hanging up when answered. By the third week, only four calls had produced people who appeared at the center. None . . . came more than once.[41]

Prior to the use of ads, Miss Kim wrote another article. This one, rather than theological like the one she had written in Oregon, was journalistic. Entitled, "Four Thousand Koreans Are Proclaiming the Advent of the Great New Age," it was sent to *Fate* and to *Chime* magazines, two New Age publications. However, as Miss Kim noted, "We had no response from the article."[42]

The last attempt at what John Lofland termed "disembodied" communication was a massive letter writing campaign undertaken at the University of California campus at Berkeley. Peter Koch, a thirty-four year old German student who had joined the movement, was concerned to reach other foreign students. Spending much of September and October, 1962, going through some 25,000 cards in the student file locating foreign students by copying off the name, address, religion (if any), and nationality of "anyone not from the U.S.," Peter sent hand signed letters to over 1,900 students. The result, as he noted, was "not very impressive."[43] Out of 150 who responded by phone, thirty-six came to hear the message. Only one joined: Edwin Ang, a Chinese student from Indonesia working on his doctorate in economics.

Summarizing these efforts, John Lofland concluded:

> One fact about these strategies is inescapable: they consistently failed to produce the results desired by the DP's. These efforts were not only failures by external criteria (no matter how low one's expectations), but, more important, they were perceived by the DP's as truly abortive. The failures became a source of threat to faith and hope that had to be managed.[44]

Basically, management took two forms. First, was the realization by the community that they lacked an adequate foundation for certain of the programs they had envisioned. Hence, time was spent improving the text, incorporating the group, obtaining a training center—maintenance and preparatory functions—until the *kairos* was right. The second response to the failure of mass-proselytization attempts was an affirmation by the community that "personal contact was the most effective way to initiate access and gain interest."[45]

Personal witness. The personalized, or what John Lofland termed the "embodied" approach led the community to witness through their jobs, in churches, and in public settings. While this proved more successful than mass communication efforts, there were still many failures, especially when the community undertook programmatic efforts to gain converts. The first of these was a decision in August, 1961, to initiate door-to-door witnessing. Miss Kim noted:

> For this purpose we had printed ID cards to be carried by members which showed their status as evangelists of HSA-UWC. We had been eager to begin this but waited until our incorporation was settled.[46]

Door-to-door canvassing was combined later in the month with door-to-door sales. Al Taylor, a salesman who had moved into the center, convinced everyone that to reach the residential areas and to master the technique of door-to-door witnessing, sales training was a must. Doris, Pauline, and Patty subsequently quit their jobs and along with Douglas Burns, a friend of George Norton's who had moved down from Oregon, went to Watkins Products to train as salesmen. Shortly afterwards, they began making appointments. The strategy, however, was short-lived. As Lofland noted,

> Within two weeks it was painfully evident that far from making a pitch after completing a sale, they were having trouble getting into homes in the first place. The group's finances began to falter without the contributions of the three women. They struggled along into September when Lee (i.e., Kim) halted the venture.[47]

Akin to the efforts of house-to-house witnessing were Miss Kim's efforts at minister visitation the following spring. Accompanied by two or more members, Miss Kim visited mainline churches virtually every day from March to May, 1962. The purpose was to offer each minister the group's latest handbill, "The New Age Has Arrived." According to John Lofland, "Most ministers did not seem to get beyond the first few lines . . . and the DP's were quickly ushered out the door."[48] Miss Kim also noted the lack of positive response:

> I . . . visited a Unitarian minister who said that he had no time to examine our message and didn't believe in apocalyptic literature. A Methodist minister told me that it would be wasting time to talk like this, because his church had its own belief . . . I had a stormy meeting with the minister of Calvary Presbyterian Church. He said that the New Testament is the final revelation and that because the goal of Christianity is different from that of other religions, unification is a wrong idea.[49]

Still impatient with the slow expansion of the movement, Doris and Pauline began street preaching at Union Square in central San Francisco. Carrying a banner with the words "Christ is on Earth,"[50] the two appeared daily between five and six o'clock along with the Salvation Army, a prophet with a sandwich board announcing the end of the world, and others. Lofland, again, noted the results:

> They found themselves quite unable to snare an audience from the flood of pedestrians, who seemed more interested in getting home than in hearing about the last days. The prophet with the sandwich board was the only person to listen to them and he had a distracting habit of walking back and forth in front of them yelling that they were anti-Christs. The situation was further complicated by another set of millennarians who sometimes got to the island before the DP's and preempted its use.[51]

No less than Miss Kim in Oregon, the community in the Bay Area, though feeling great responsibility, was helpless in many ways. Every systematic attempt of their own to spread the message and expand the movement had ended in failure. It was clear that the Bay Area was not going to convert *en masse* to the

Principle, and in this context, the group's expectations began to be modified. Rather than all-at-once hopes, members saw that they would have to win people one by one into the New Age. This modification of expectation was also reflected in a modification of proselytization techniques: as members found it more effective and realistic to meet people, at least initially, less on an ideological than on a personal or human level. This, in one sense, required a greater amount of sensitivity to the realities of a given situation. When such sensitivity was lacking, this approach resulted in charges of deception.[52] In any case, given the historical circumstances, this approach became prevalent.

Conversion-promotion techniques

As Lofland noted, strategies of access merely secured interested persons or prospects. This was only the "rudimentary first step," after which "the DP's . . . could get on with the real work of promoting conversion." Contrasting the group's recruitment practices with more sophisticated church bodies, Lofland maintained,

> While the DP's engaged in considerable promotion activity, their procedures were not systematized. Promotion was in many respects haphazard and dependent upon the inclination of adherents at any given moment. This variableness is most acutely indicated by the DP's extremely limited vocabulary for referring to differential prospect alignments. . . . Thus almost all prospects were lumped together as either "interested people," "new people," "students," "material," or sometimes even "prospects."
> Likewise, discernable promotion vehicles and tactics often lacked designative terms. The enterprise was conducted in the style of a group of amateurs haltingly but seriously playing the game of winning souls.[53]

Despite underdeveloped and variable approaches to the question of recruitment, Lofland noted that the "DP's" utilized "two concrete promotion vehicles . . . the 'briefing session'. . . (and) the 'study group' or meeting."

The "briefing session." What Lofland termed the briefing session consisted of an introductory presentation of the Principle to an interested guest or guests. In February, 1961, the group made a tape recording of the lecture which not only standardized the presentation but also made for a degree of flexibility. As Miss Kim noted,

> Because we had taped the lectures, we invited people to come whenever they could. Often they would come during the day—even in the morning. Sometimes we had three tapes of different chapters playing in separate rooms.[54]

At the same time, there were problems with the taped lectures. The chief of these was length. Lofland wrote:

> Lee [i.e., Kim], anxious to make certain that the initial picture given was an adequate one, abbreviated the DP book only slightly, and when recorded . . . it ran four and a half hours. Elmer [i.e., George Norton] set up a tape recorder in the scene room, where visiting prospects were taken and left alone to listen. Not surprisingly, DP's found that few people would sit four and a half hours listening to a tape recording. They tended to walk out without a word after an hour or so or to excuse themselves, claiming the press of other business. Sometimes the tape would finish and the DP's entered the room only to find the prospect sound asleep. Eventually the recording was split into two segments of about two hours each, and an attempt was made to have people come to separate sittings. This of course posed the problem of getting anyone to return.[55]

According to John Lofland, "The four and a half hour format endured for eight months before it was at last agreed that it was too long." At that point, it was reduced to two and a half hours, and six months later, to an hour and twenty minutes. Six minutes more were shortly to be pared off. Finally, in November, 1963, Miss Kim reduced the tape to thirty-four minutes.

Again, the motivating factor behind this progression was the reality of their situation. Just as in witnessing, the group found that even an interested person could not digest the Principle at one sitting. At the same time, they saw that doctrine alone was not enough to inspire conversion, but that affective bonds were required. Shortening the tape and adopting the practice of sitting in the room during the session to answer questions or clarify points were attempts to deal with these problems.

The "study group." Once a guest had expressed interest in the Principle, that person was invited to participate in the study group. There, the attempt was made to integrate affective bonds with an understanding of the Principle. Guests shared in song, prayer, and fellowship as well as in the serial reading of the Principle. Still, there were problems. John Lofland noted:

> The study group was designed to lead a set of persons from the beginning to the end of the DP book. The ideal pace was to study one chapter a meeting, two meetings a week for six weeks. This projected course was rarely realized. Only a handful of people attended that often or that long. The course was frequently started for new people, who would then drop out; new people would come, and the book would be started over; they would drop out, and so forth.[56]

The opposite problem was with those who persisted interminably in study groups without casting their lot with the community. Again, as Lofland noted,

What a person should do with his life in view of the
DP was so obvious, they thought, that it need not even
be spoken.

Therefore, when confronted with prospects who
had all the information and were still disinclined to give
themselves over, DP's were at a loss as to what to do
next . . .DP's were likewise at a loss in dealing with
verbal converts. Those people knew the situation and
apparently believed in it, but inexplicably held back.[57]

Despite the limitations in recruitment practices the group
slowly began to grow. During the eighteen months that the
community lived together in San Francisco (first at Cole Street
and then at Masonic Avenue), at least eleven new people moved
into the "center."[58] While most of these were temporary
occupants, several had become bona-fide residents by the time
the community radically altered the direction of its mission.

Bay Area and Beyond

The group radically altered its center life in July, 1962 by
dispersing to various cities throughout the Bay Area. Miss Kim
reflected on that decision in her memoirs:

We decided to open up mission territory in the suburbs
and communities around San Francisco. We had been
wanting to expand our work. All of us wanted to go out
to new cities and thus spread the message widely . . .
Now we had purchased a house and several members
lived at the Masonic center. We could maintain it and
carry on our work, spiritually as well as financially. As
soon as the remodeling work was finished, I called a
meeting. They were eager to go out.[59]

Not surprisingly, Miss Kim's recollection was at variance
with John Lofland's report of the event:

On July 3, Lee [i.e., Kim] assembled converts for a
family meeting, at which time she laid it on the line.
She was getting tired of working with people who did
not work more swiftly. She threatened to leave and start
work someplace else with a new group, because she
was getting tired of "looking at the same old faces" and
wanted to see new people. A choice was set: converts
had to go out and start new works in neighboring
towns, or else she was leaving. More than that, it was
time that converts proved themselves by going out and
working alone.[60]

Undoubtedly, both reflections were true. The group had
wanted to expand the mission and, at the same time, was
frustrated with the lack of progress. Regardless of the
motivation, the decision was made. Doris left for San Jose on
July 6th. Pauline departed for Berkeley on the 10th. Patty went
to Hayward on the 17th, and Galen left for Burlingame on the
20th. George Norton remained at San Francisco headquarters to
assist Miss Kim.

For the purposes of gaining membership, the dispersion
through the Bay Area was a constructive step. In the second
eighteen months that Miss Kim's group spent in the Bay Area,
at least eighteen new members joined as well as numerous
associates. The dispersion led also to the institution (or
re-institution) of the monthly newsletter, Miss Kim's frequent
circuit rides, and the weekend training session.

The Newsletter

The monthly newsletter which Miss Kim last typed and sent
out from Eugene, Oregon, in November, 1960, was re-instituted
in September, 1963. As she noted,

Once again we needed a newsletter, since now we had
opened outlying centers in San Jose, Berkeley, Burlingame, and Hayward. A newsletter would be helpful

to keep everyone in touch with other members and their
activities. I typed newsletter number three on the 9th.
. . . We continued our monthly newsletter from then
on.[61]

Entitled *New Age Frontiers*, this monthly newsletter was the
official periodical of Miss Kim's group until 1973. During these
ten years, its format changed little. Miss Kim wrote:

> I edited letters which members sent and translated
> Korean and Japanese news from letters and magazines.
> I included articles based on the books I had read and
> put in what educational material I could find to broaden
> the members and to equip them to deal with the
> questions of their students.[62]

As members pursued missionary activities in various locales,
a significant portion of each newsletter was devoted to "letters
from the field." In these letters, members shared reports of
recent witnessing activities, testimonies of new converts, and
general news. According to John Lofland, the letters were
equally important as a medium for expressions of love and
devotion:

> In some ways it (the newsletter) seemed to be a more
> effective underpinning of faith than simply living
> together. The newsletter gave permanent expression to
> devotional vocalizing, resolutions to work, and
> admonitions to persevere. DP's frequently re-read their
> accumulated issues and seemed to gain new inspiration
> each time. The oral is ephemeral, but the written can
> become sacred and a source of ever-renewed faith. [63]

Not only did the newsletter connect Miss Kim's group but
also, through her translations of letters from Korea and Japan,
it solidified a connection to the international movement. Under
"News from Korea," Miss Kim reported regularly on the 40-day

Enlightenment movements during which a reported 6,000 volunteers evangelized the country villages of South Korea. Beginning in December, 1963, Miss Kim also began to report "News from the Japanese Family." During that month, several young leaders from Risshokoseikai, a large Buddhist sect, converted, summoned 150 district youth leaders to hear the Principles, and ordered 3,000 books. The following spring, she reported on the Japanese family's contact with Mr. Takahashi, head of the Kotonari Shinto sect and tutor to the Royal Family.[64]

Besides relating to events within the Unification movement, the newsletter also connected members to Christian and non-Christian religious traditions. Synopses of Gospel commentaries were included in successive months, and Miss Kim also devoted a substantial amount of space to a comparative exposition of major world religions. In addition to explicitly educational materials, most newsletters began with one of Miss Kim's sermons. These usually combined millennial sentiments with tough-minded pragmatism. Typical titles were "Heaven Is the Kingdom of Use," "Let us Expand the Territory of Good," "How Does the New World Start?" and "Wisdom, Sober Judgment."[65]

Circuit Rider

The newsletter was not the only connecting point for members in the Bay Area following expansion. Another was Miss Kim herself. Dispersion to disparate locales in the Bay Area was a signal for her to begin the circuit rides that had characterized her mission work in Oregon. Unlike Oregon, however, Miss Kim this time had members at her stops and a driver, George Norton. As early as August 5, 1962, while visiting several guests of Doris in San Jose, she set up the basic pattern for these rides: leave San Francisco at 2:30 p.m., help prepare for the evening gathering, speak following the tape, and arrive back at San Francisco at 1:30 a.m.[66]

Berkeley and San Jose were the most active centers, and Miss Kim met new members at each. By December, 1962, her trips were coordinated so that she visited San Jose on Tuesdays and Berkeley on Thursdays. Although activities were somewhat curtailed during that month by proofreading the third edition of the Principle text, by January, the Berkeley center contacted Emilia Rathbun, and Palo Alto became a regular stop also. An excerpt from Miss Kim's memoirs, dated March 1962, captures the flavor of her travels:

> Each of the women in Emilia's group held gatherings in their homes, and some invited me to come and teach. During the month I taught a group of three in San Mateo and nine women in San Carlos. I also traveled to Galen's house in Burlingame to teach. Gordon's mother and two friends had studied with Gordon. I went to Los Altos and studied with them. I went to Emilia's once again and, of course, to San Jose and Berkeley.

Training Session

Although Miss Kim's visits continued unabated into early spring, by May, 1963, they were replaced by a new development, the training session. Rather than have Miss Kim go out to the various centers, the centers began to bring guests to headquarters. This innovation first occurred the previous December when five people from San Jose came up for a short training session. A month later, Doris brought two more students up, but it wasn't until May that the first official training session was held. Miss Kim wrote:

> We held our first formal training session on Friday, Saturday, and Sunday, the 3rd, 4th, and 5th. Members gathered from all centers to attend. Some arrived Friday night. On Saturday morning members took

physical exercise together, cleaned the house, and
began to practice lecturing.[67]

Intended for members, it was almost by accident that the
group found that the "training session" was a viable recruiting
device for new people as well. Miss Kim noted:

> Ernie Stewart attended. He had responded to an ad. . .
> in the paper. . . . At the training session I lectured
> chapters one through six. Ernie was fascinated. We had
> two hours of testimony in the afternoon, and in the
> evening Joe Mason taught chapters seven through
> twelve. On Sunday everyone practiced lecturing.[68]

The training session made both the briefing session and the
study group obsolete as recruitment devices. With members
learning how to lecture, the impersonal tape could be discarded,
and by collapsing all twelve chapters of the Principle into one
weekend session, the protracted study group was no longer
necessary. Combining lectures with fellowship and testimonies,
the training session was an intensely potent experience.
Recognizing its potential, the group quickly held two more
training sessions in May. They finally had found a viable
recruitment device.

Crisis

Although prospects brightened for Bay Area expansion
during the first six months of 1963, there were also several
threatening developments. Miss Kim learned in March that Col.
Bo Hi Pak had incorporated a separate association in Arlington,
Virginia and had applied for a federal tax exemption ahead of
her. Also in that month, she heard that John Lofland was
continuing his investigation by contacting people whose names
he had copied from the center guest book. In April, as noted,
Miss Kim found out that her visa application had been lost for

a year and, on inquiring, was given thirty days to reapply or leave the country. Then, though not exactly a threat, the community was at least depleted by the departure of five members in May and June to mission fields outside the Bay Area. Peter Koch and Ursula Schumann left for Germany. Douglas Burns, now a two-year member, left the San Francisco center for Fresno on the 8th, and on the 22nd, Doris Walder and Orah Schoon left San Jose to begin mission work in Los Angeles.

As disruptive as any of these developments may have been, the major crisis of the period was a severe appendicitis attack suffered by Miss Kim. More critical than any deportation proceedings, Miss Kim recalled the June episode in her memoirs:

> On the 28th a pain began on my right side, and I threw up quite a lot. On the 29th I went to Oakland and taught a group. . . . The pain intensified. I arrived home about midnight and the pain became extremely severe. I slept only about two hours, and awoke. The pain was almost unbearable. In desperation I called George at work and had him paged at 4:00 a.m. He couldn't have known my state, and reasoned that there was little to be done at that hour since everyone was asleep. He said that he would come home at 7:30 and advised me to take some Pepto-Bismol to soothe my stomach. When George came back he tried to get doctors he knew, but none were available. Finally, Dr. Kim, a Korean physician, was recommended. He came at 11:00 and examined me. He said that it was appendicitis and that it was very late. He said there was no time to call an ambulance and that we must leave immediately. He drove us to the Presbyterian Medical Center where I was operated on from 12:00 p.m. to 2:00 p.m. I awoke five hours later. It had been necessary to cleanse the intestine since my appendix had ruptured. He said that it was almost too late and that I must have had "heavenly luck" to have survived.[69]

Success

The group suffered a near tragedy in the appendicitis attack of Miss Kim. Yet, in many ways, her illness was the last storm of many the group had absorbed since transplanting themselves from Oregon to the Bay Area. Having come successfully out of this last one, Miss Kim and the group reaped abundantly in the next few months. Not only did Miss Kim win her long awaited immigrant's visa, but the group received favorable news in its quest for a Federal tax exemption. In addition, the community received the long awaited copies of the third edition of *The Divine Principles*.

More importantly, the group reaped a full harvest of new converts. Pauline Phillips, who had moved to Sacramento, brought John and Sandi Pinkerton to the Principle. The Pinkertons, in turn, brought Paul and Christel Werner, a German couple who were living in Sacramento with their son Klaus. Galen Pumphrey, in Burlingame, witnessed to Jim Fleming, a former neighbor of his from Kansas, and his wife, Mary, both of whom were members of the Yokefellows Interdenominational Christian fellowship. Gordon Ross brought Lowell Martin, a junior executive from Oakland. Nor was the Bay Area the only locale for recruitment. Doris and Orah were winning new people in Los Angeles, including Teddy Verheyan who sent a large financial contribution of his entire savings. Joe Mason, a member from San Jose who had been drafted, brought Philip Burley, a fellow soldier at Fort Sill, Oklahoma.

All of these people came together in November 1963 for "Children's Day," one of three holidays instituted by the movement.[70] The entire fruit of Miss Kim's and her group's three-year effort in the Bay Area assembled at Masonic Avenue for the November 16th celebration. Philip Burley, the soldier from Fort Sill, obtained a leave and flew in on the 13th. Three young men who had been studying the Principle in Los Angeles hitchhiked to San Jose and walked the rest of the way to San Francisco. Other Los Angeles members and students arrived on the 14th. Teddy Verheyan's roommate came from Los Angeles on a bicycle and arrived on the 15th. On that same day, members arrived from Fresno and Sacramento. At last, Masonic Avenue center was filled! Miss Kim described the celebration:

> Twenty-four people met at midnight on the 16th for special prayer and ceremony for Children's Day. For the day's celebration, fifty-one people gathered. It was such a joy to see carload after carload of people arriving. Some had been like isolated lights here and there. Now they were coming together, and it was like a bonfire. New members were introduced and gave their testimonies. Old members could meet again and share their many new experiences. It was like a happy family reunion, one that didn't center only in the past, but was actively planning the future. We heard local reports from Los Angeles, Sacramento, Berkeley, Fremont, Burlingame, Oakland, Fresno, San Jose, and Oklahoma. We ate turkey dinner together, gave personal testimonies, and saw Philip's slides of Korea. We closed after midnight.[71]

The 1963 Children's Day celebration was long remembered by participants. Yet if it was a culmination of three years work in the Bay Area, it was also a turning point. Prior to the celebration, at the annual meeting of the Board for the election of officers, Miss Kim decided to resign from the presidency and recommended Gordon Ross who was elected. With a new president, new membership, and new books, everyone looked to a new future. That future, however, was different than any of them could have imagined. Within a short time, events occurred which completely altered the course of the Bay Area story.

NOTES

1. Kim, *Memoirs,* January 1961.
2. Ibid.
3. Ibid.
4. For a description of Williams College (under the pseudonym, Amhurst College), see Lofland, *Doomsday Cult,* 69.
5. Kim, *Memoirs,* July 1961.
6. Kim, *Memoirs,* July 1963.
7. Lofland, *Doomsday Cult,* 139; Kim, Memoirs. July 1961
8. Lofland, *Doomsday Cult,* 70.
9. Kim, *Memoirs,* January 1961.
10. Lofland, *Doomsday Cult,* 71-72.
11. Kim, *Memoirs,* June 1961; Lofland, *Doomsday Cult,* 155-161.
12. Kim, *Memoirs,* September 1961.
13. Kim, *Memoirs,* January 1963.
14. Pauline Phillips, "News from Berkeley," *New Age Frontiers,* January 15 1963.
15. Young Oon Kim, "Suffering Is a Privilege," *New Age Frontiers,* October 10, 1963.
16. Kim, *Memoirs,* February 1962.
17. Ibid.
18. Ibid .
19. Gordon Ross, "News from Berkeley," *New Age Frontiers,* December 15, 1963.
20. Pauline Phillips, "News from Berkeley," *New Age Frontiers,* December 15, 1962.
21. Bo Hi Pak, "News from Arlington, Va.," *New Age Frontiers,* May 15, 1963.
22. Kim, *Memoirs,* March 1963.
23. See Lofland, *Doomsday Cult,* 76.
24. Kim, *Memoirs,* June 1962.
25. Kim, *Memoirs,* January 1963.
26. Lofland, *Doomsday Cult,* 274.
27. John Lofland, "Reflection on my First Year with the Divine Principles," *New Age Frontiers,* January 15, 1963, 7.

28. Kim, *Memoirs,* June, 1963.

29. *Doomsday Cult* went through six printings from 1966-75 and was republished in an enlarged edition by Irvington in 1977.

30. Lofland, *Doomsday Cult, 8.*

31. Ibid., 8-9.

32. Ibid., 248. According to Lofland, "In the mid-seventies, people began frequently to guess and assert that the 'DPs' were the newly famous Moonies." Into the early eighties, Lofland acknowledged that his 'secret' had become "absurdly obvious" and in 1983 he asked the president of the Unification Church in America to release him from the agreement of anonymity he had promised in 1962. Lofland states, "The president granted my request and agreed, further, that only the organization and its founder required reference by their actual names. All other participants would be identified only in terms of their movement positions." (see John Lofland, Protest, New Brunswick, N.J.: Transaction, 1985, 120-21)

33. Kim, *Memoirs,* Dec. 1962

34. Lofland, *Doomsday Cult,* 72.

35. Kim, *Memoirs,* September 1961

36. Lofland, *Doomsday Cult,* 73.

37. Lofland, Ibid. 28

38. Ibid., 78-79.

39. Ibid., 69.

40. Ibid., 80.

41. Ibid., 84.

42. Kim, *Memoirs,* December 1961.

43. Peter Koch, "News from Berkeley," *New Age Frontiers,* December 5, 1972; Lofland, *Doomsday Cult,* 87.

44. Lofland, *Doomsday Cult,* 89.

45. Ibid., 84.

46. Kim, *Memoirs,* August 1961.

47. Lofland, *Doomsday Cult,* 117.

48. Lofland, *Doomsday Cult,* 111

49. Kim, *Memoirs,* March and April 1962.

50. Ibid, May 1962.

51. Lofland, *Doomsday Cult,* 117-118.

52. Lofland refers to this as "covert presentation." See Lofland, *Doomsday Cult,* 91-108.

53. Ibid., 120-121.

54. Kim, *Memoirs,* March 1961.

55. Lofland, *Doomsday Cult,* 125.

56. Ibid., 129-130.

57. Ibid., 186.

58. Kim, *Memoirs,* January 1961-July 1962.

59. Ibid., July 1962.

60. Lofland, *Doomsday Cult,* 253.

61. Kim, *Memoirs,* September 1962.

62. Ibid.

63. Lofland, *Doomsday Cult,* 234.

64. "News from Japan," *New Age Frontiers,* April 15, 1963.

65. *New Age Frontiers,* September 15 and December 15, 1962; April 15 and November 15 1963.

66. Kim, *Memoirs,* August 1962.

67. Kim, Ibid. May 1963.

68. Ibid, May 1963.

69. Ibid., June 1963.

70. The others were Parents' Day and World Day. The church's most important holiday, God's Day, began on January 1, 1968.

71. Kim, *Memoirs,* November 1963.

CHAPTER THREE

EXODUS : 1964–65

Local Changes—Prediction of Economic Collapse—Sir Anthony Brooke—Community Style—Rev. Moon Visits America—The World Tour—Back to the Bay Area

The years 1964 to 1965 were years of transition for the Unification Church in the San Francisco Bay Area. The most important transition during this period was the dispersion of the original Oakhill community. By January, 1966, none of them were left in the Bay Area. Each had moved on to new mission fields. The Pumphreys and George Norton were in Denver, Colorado. Pauline Phillips was in Cleveland, Ohio. Doris Walder was in Rome, Italy, and Miss Kim was in Washington, D.C.

In addition, many of those who had gathered for the 1963 Children's Day celebration were elsewhere. Gordon Ross was pioneering Dallas, Texas. The Werners went back to Germany, then Austria. Douglas Burns moved first from Fresno to Phoenix with Orah Schoon and then to New Orleans. Carl Rapkins was in Tampa, Florida, Sandi Pinkerton was on her way to England,and Teddy Verheyen was in Holland. The Flemings were in Washington, D.C. with Miss Kim. In short, the foundation that the Oakhill group had established in the Bay Area was broken down and scattered across the United States and Western Europe.

The causes and local effects of this diaspora were half of the story of the Unification Church in the San Francisco Bay Area during this period. The other half involved the interplay between the Bay Area church and developments in the rest of the movement. Foundations had been established in Korea and Japan as well, and the whole movement appeared to be at a point of transition. In Korea, a three-year course of 40-day "Enlightenment" movements was completed and had covered the entire peninsula.[1] In Japan, Mr. Nishikawa (Sang Ik Choi), the Unification Church missionary there, had also established a foundation also and, like Miss Kim, had recommended that a native member take over as president of the national church. By Children's Day, 1964, both Miss Kim and Mr. Choi were in Seoul, Korea. Beginning the following February, they, along with Mrs. Won Pak Choi, accompanied Rev. Moon on his first world tour, the first stop of which outside the Orient was the San Francisco Bay Area.

Thus, both local and overseas developments shaped the character of the Bay Area church during this transitional phase. Following the world tour, when Miss Kim decided to relocate in Washington, D.C., a new story was ready to unfold in the Bay Area and elsewhere. Before examining these developments, it is necessary to consider the transition period itself.

Local Changes

The first changes that affected the Bay Area church during this period were organizational. Having recommended Gordon Ross as her successor, Miss Kim was no longer president of HSA-UWC. This transition was significant, especially given the role she had played in the community's development. Obviously, it would be difficult, if not impossible, to replace Miss Kim as the leader of the association, especially while she was still in the vicinity. There were several conflicts. One of the first and most serious was Gordon's proposal to rewrite the Principle text. Given her constant work, this was a sore spot for Miss Kim, and she noted, "This was very presumptuous of him." At the same time, she had begun to suspect the new president's motives:

> He had many years to go to become a trustworthy and dependable leader. . . . I had made Gordon the president simply to train him, but this he never understood.[2]

While difficulties are to be expected in any organizational transition, the problems which confronted HSA-UWC were complicated by cross-cultural and religious issues. Miss Kim, after all, was Rev. Moon's direct representative. While she may have relinquished organizational authority, she by no means had relinquished spiritual authority, as evidenced in her attitude toward the new president. At the same time, it was this split between organizational and spiritual authority that brought about a breakdown of community and general exodus. As long as Miss Kim had been able to fulfill both functions, the community had held together. Now that she had relinquished organizational authority, her spiritual authority also began to be questioned. Not only were her views overridden on at least one occasion, but Miss Kim, herself, seemed to be influenced by the more 'spiritual' members of the community. More erratic prophecies and hopes were again articulated, and members, at their own inspiration, began to be called to new mission fields. Those who remained or joined in the Bay Area adopted a community style radically different than before.

Prediction of Economic Collapse

It is difficult to overestimate the significance of President John Kennedy's assassination on November 22, 1963. In some respects, it was a shocking conclusion to the conservatism of the 1950s and an abrupt beginning to the radical turmoil of the 1960s. For the Bay Area Unification Church, the turn of events, so tantalizingly close to the election of their new president, re-awakened earlier feelings of being a saved remnant. This time, however, rather than looking for the nation to convert *en masse*, the group sensed an imminent disaster.

Mary Fleming, who, along with her husband, was given to receiving messages through disembodied spirit friends, began intuiting "an economic collapse in America." The first message came shortly after the Kennedy assassination. She received the second message on "the coming economic collapse" on November 28, 1963, and the community began to mobilize. Miss Kim wrote:

> We held a training session on the 30th and discussed preparations for the collapse. According to the message the dollar would be devaluated completely and all money would be worthless. Therefore, it would be necessary to convert our money to food and usable goods while there was still time. There was some support for this gloomy economic outlook in the press, but to me this extreme prediction sounded very strange.
> . . . I suggested that rather than buying up food, we should deposit our money in a Swiss bank and wait out whatever economic crisis arose. Mary received that this was a wise idea, but that eventually the Swiss franc would also be affected. Nevertheless, I was in favor of depositing. The members, however, were fully expectant of catastrophe. I didn't force my view on them, so we didn't deposit in the Swiss bank, but began buying great quantities of food.[3]

It was significant that although Miss Kim urged characteristic caution, members overruled her and opted for the more radical alternative of stocking the Masonic Avenue house basement with food. Miss Kim, herself, appeared to have been caught up in the general expectation by January 1st. In her New Year's sermon of 1964, "Our Time Has Come!" she wrote:

> When the economy collapses how many ministers
> will remain in their posts to preach the gospel? Without
> a car, without pay, will they still be inspired to preach
> the grace of God? Maria Elliot, a Portuguese spiritualist
> and a former actress, has accepted the Divine Principle,
> and recently she received a message for me in which
> she saw a huge beautiful eagle, flying in a dark sky.
> Then the eagle tumbled. . . .
> The Christian Church is no longer supported by
> spirit and truth but has been maintained in the last few
> decades by the power of the dollar. When the dollar is
> taken away, the eagle will tumble and the church will
> also lose its last foundation.[4]

The economic crisis, however, did not occur in early 1964
as predicted. The messages' impact was far less on the economy
than on the small community of believers in the Bay Area.
Rather than the dollar, it was the community that collapsed, and
a general exodus of members from the Bay Area to new locales
of missionary endeavor began. By far, the most significant
departures were those of the community's two presidents.
Gordon Ross, after leading several street preaching efforts at
Union Square, left for Dallas, Texas, in late January. Miss Kim,
permanent visa in hand, left the Bay Area for a visit to Korea in
late February. Although her visit lasted eleven months and left
the Bay Area effectively rudderless during that time, Miss Kim
met a singular person before departing.

Sir Anthony Brooke

Former Rajah Muda of Sarawak in northern Borneo, Sir
Anthony Brooke represented the culmination of the Bay Area
church's interaction with the New Age milieu. A quixotic figure
born into a line of 'white rajahs' ruling Sarawak from 1841 until
1946 when it became a British colony, Anthony had "led" the
populace in "defying the British government, and even the King

of England." Continuing his quixotic efforts, he subsequently became the leader of an English metaphysical group and traveled constantly, promoting global consciousness and the "Universal Link Revelation."[5]

In Los Angeles, Brooke met Doris Walder, became excited about the Principle, and immediately flew to San Francisco where he met with Miss Kim who was about to leave for Korea. Excited even more, he quickly made plans to join her there. His decision to go is best described in his own words:

> I found myself being drawn by a seemingly irresistible force to Korea and to the presence of Sun Myung Moon, but not before I had received a direct inward intimation that Sun Myung Moon was in a particular sense the "earth form of Limitless Love." It was in these precise words that I found myself giving recognition to him as I awakened in the early hours before a California dawn with every fibre of my being aglow. . . . I became increasingly convinced that the role of Sun Myung Moon would be progressively recognized by mankind as having unique significance not merely for the peoples of the East but for the whole of humanity in relationship to the leadership of the new age and in connection with the events foretold in the Universal Link Revelation.[6]

In Korea, with Miss Kim translating, Brooke spoke before 800 people at a correctional institution, 2,000 people at Citizens' Hall, and on Korean national television. Leaving Korea, he arranged for a brief speaking tour covering Osaka, Kyoto, Hiroshima,and Tokyo in Japan before arriving back in San Francisco on April 10, 1964. Lofland wrote "DP's who met him at the airport rejoiced in his disembarking exclamation: 'It's true! It's all gloriously true!'"[7]

Conceiving his mission to be that of "coordinating revelations," Anthony visited new Unification centers in Los Angeles, Denver, Oklahoma, Dallas,and Cleveland as well as

Col. Pak's group in Washington, D.C., before returning to England in May. He also met leaders of the Unity School in Kansas and clairvoyant, Arthur Ford, with whom he did a 'reading' that was to circulate widely. In England, he established links with several spiritual groups that subsequently made reference to the name Sun Myung Moon in their newsletters of 1964. Finally, in November, Sir Anthony Brooke returned to Sarawak for the first time in twenty years and "witnessed to the new revelation."[8] His contact with the Unification Church continued for several years.

Community Style

The community style that developed in the Bay Area during this period of transition was quite different from what had gone before. The most obvious difference was that those who remained were relatively leaderless. This leaderless state was, perhaps, best reflected in a succession of weekend meetings following Miss Kim's departure. The first, on March 3, 1964, was guided by Jim Fleming from Burlingame. The second, a week later, was under the direction of Edwin Ang of Berkeley. The third, on the 17th, was chaired by Lowell Martin of Oakland, and the fourth, on the 24th, was conducted by Sandi Pinkerton from Sacramento.

Although Miss Kim planned only to visit Korea, her return was repeatedly delayed. She had wanted to return in May, but Rev. Moon restrained her. By mid-June, she still had not returned. She wrote,

> When I think of each one of you, I feel urgent and am anxious to return to you. At the same time, I have an important part to play in the work here. . . .
>
> It is necessary for me to stay away from you for a while to see how you carry on the work. God is planning important things for each of you, and it is absolutely necessary to go through a certain period by

yourselves. So don't think foolish things or complain;
just work hard with faith and gratitude. My thoughts go
to you and are with you more than they are here.[9]

By October, Miss Kim was no longer issuing challenges but
counseling endurance:

In your troubled times, you can manifest your capa-
bility, faithfulness, loyalty, and wisdom. So everything
will work out for the good. I will return soon and see
you all.[10]

At the same time, it is important to recognize that, despite
difficulties, Bay Area members were not despairing. The crisis
of local organization was not a crisis of faith. On the contrary,
Bay Area members felt that whatever members they had lost to
other locales, the message was spreading. Hence, there was
hope. Everyone was simply a missionary again— the Martins in
Oakland, the Pinkertons in Sacramento, Edwin Ang in Berkeley
and the Flemings in Burlingame. As John Pinkerton put it, "1964
is the year of expansion."[11]

In the context of movement expansion and their own
organizational depletion, the role of the Bay Area church became
that of a clearing house for news. With the increase in the
volume of letters and news from missionaries in the field, more
and more time was focused on the newsletter. The decision to
publish the *New Age Frontiers* twice monthly further inhibited
local outreach. As Jim Fleming wrote,

The San Francisco Center Family have threatened to
get a rubber stamp for their news section each issue
which reads as follows: "News from San Francisco: We
have been busy getting out the Newsletter."[12]

Additionally, the San Francisco center began charging
subscription rates and investigated obtaining a copyright. In
October, 1964, a copyright was obtained for the newsletter in the

name of the "Unified Family" rather than the Unification Church, a choice that would have future ramifications.[13]

Aside from its frequency and format, the content of the newsletter also changed. Most obvious were the opening messages. Whereas Miss Kim had been able to balance millennialist visions with a tough-minded pragmatism, the new editors were entirely visionary. Miss Kim's sermons were replaced by messages from spirit world friends whose themes were less evangelistic witness than personal growth.[14]

This arcane and eclectic approach to the newsletter was manifested in evangelistic activities which featured less street witnessing than a kind of "mail-order" proselytization. While confined to her home because of illness, Mary Fleming constructed a correspondence course "to enlighten someone who did not have a Principle teacher within their vicinity."Drawing material from many sources" including diagrams Gordon Ross first introduced and descriptions Miss Kim and others used, she reported having "sixteen people participating in the course from distances as far away as Bechuanaland, Africa. Significant here was the current Bay Area group's avowedly eclectic re-working of the Principle. As a result of the correspondence course, two couples in St. Louis professed conversion and joined.[15]

Although would be unfair to say that Bay Area activities were limited to 'literary' efforts—witnessing continued—still the overall character of the Bay Area group had changed. Unlike the original Oakhill group which had severed ties with family, jobs, and locales, the current Bay Area community gave more the impression of pursuing the Principle within the context of already existing families and careers. Jim Fleming and Lowell Martin were businessmen, and Edwin Ang was working on his doctoral dissertation at the University of California at Berkeley. In this respect, concerns that would have been alien to Miss Kim's original group were now voiced. A good example was the concern expressed in *New Age Frontiers* for Sheeba, the Flemings' four year old dachshund:

> To those of you who knew and prayed for Sheeba's
> recovery from paralysis, our grateful thanks! Sheeba...
> ruptured a disc in her spine eight weeks ago and was
> completely paralyzed on the back end. The day she first
> wagged her tail again was a great one, and there has
> been steady improvement since. She has not completely
> regained her coordination yet, but she is functioning
> very adequately, thank you.[16]

In many ways, the local group took on the attributes of any
number of groups of the occult milieu. Those who joined in the
Bay Area during this period were mainly middle-aged and older
women.[17] Excitement was less over new prospects than over
visits from other members. In short, the Bay Area was largely
inactive. Moreover, it was clear that the impetus for new
developments was to come not from within but from without. In
this context, changes in the movement as a whole played a
decisive role.

As previously mentioned, the situations leading to dispersion
and the local effects of that dispersion constitute only one half of
the story of the Unification Church in the San Francisco Bay
Area during this period. The other, and in many ways more
significant half, related to the Bay Area church's interplay with
developments in the rest of the movement. Whereas members
learned of these developments second hand via the newsletter in
1964, this knowledge became decidedly first hand in 1965.

Reverend Moon Visits America

In all stages of its development, the American church
anticipated the imminent arrival of Rev. Moon. Miss Kim had
expected his arrival with David S.C. Kim in 1959 and out of her
meager funds rented an apartment and purchased bedding and
other items. The original Oakhill group in the Bay Area
anticipated his arrival in the spring of 1961 and purchased a
camper. This same expectation was a focus of the 1964 Bay Area

community. They, along with members throughout the country, began a "High Noon Prayer Vigil" in anticipation, and by November, word came through the *New Age Frontiers* that "Time is growing short."[18] This time they were not disappointed.

Rev. Moon departed from Korea for his first world tour in January, 1965. After spending two weeks in Japan, he and Mrs. Won Pak Choi left for America. Miss Kim, who accompanied them to Japan, departed ahead of them "to prepare Americans for his visit."[19] In an article, "Hail to the Brightness," the *New Age Frontiers* chronicled Rev. Moon's San Francisco Bay Area arrival:

> The Great Day dawned for us before the sun was up. At 5:30 a.m. on the still, cool morning of Friday, February 12th, our Master set foot upon the continent of North America. Twenty-seven highly honored, greatly privileged, and totally breathless members of the Unified Family in the United States were on hand to greet him and Mrs. Choi as they stepped off the Japan Airlines flight from Hawaii at the San Francisco International Airport. Among the fortunate few were the three missionaries from Korea whose love and single-minded devotion were responsible for the presence of Americans at the momentous occasion—Miss Young Oon Kim, Col. Bo Hi Pak, and Mr. David Kim.[20]

As "West Coast Headquarters" had been transferred to the 1139 Wellington address of the Martins in Oakland, the "Official Party" stayed at the Oakland center for the seven days they remained in the San Francisco Bay Area. There were meetings every night during which Rev. Moon spoke, and answered questions. Days were spent showing the visitors "points of interest in and around San Francisco." Yet neither lecturing nor sightseeing were the primary focus of Rev. Moon's visit. As reported in the *New Age Frontiers*,

The high point of the Master's visit in the San
Francisco area was the selection and sanctification of
Sacred Ground. The site was chosen on February 14th,
and the ceremony took place on the 15th. This will be
Holy Ground for all members in this area, and has
already been the scene of several meetings for prayer
and renewal.[21]

The first "Holy Ground" established by Rev. Moon in the
United States was on Twin Peaks overlooking San Francisco. In
the next forty-four days, Rev. Moon traveled by car to all
forty-eight continental United States setting up a total of fifty-five
Holy Grounds. A key part of each ceremony was the burying of
a "holy rock" from Korea. Having completed a three year course
of "national restoration" on the Korean peninsula, Rev. Moon
transplanted Korean rocks in American soil. At the same time,
a pebble was gathered from the grounds of City Hall at each stop
in America and put into a sack for later transport to Korea.

While individual Holy Ground sites were selected on the
basis of setting and the possibility of public access, the directions
to several of the Holy Grounds, such as the second one in Los
Angeles, read more like treasure maps:

Griffith Park: Enter from Fern Dell Dr., pass vertical
parking area on right & picnic ground #7 to parking
area on right. Walk past men's rest room #4 & picnic
area. Go up dirt pathway to left of picnic area to where
large dirt road turns left and steeper trail goes up to
right of picnic area. Take steeper path. Climb past
small water faucet with spigot about 72 paces. Holy
Ground is on plateau 6 paces from middle of trail.[22]

Heading east across the country, ground was blessed at the
highest point (Mt. Whitney) and the lowest point (Death Valley)
in the United States. Col. Pak joined the Official Party in Florida
and traveled north with them to Washington, D.C., where the
twenty-fifth and twenty-sixth Holy Grounds were blessed: the

first at the Ellipse behind the White House and the second, on the lawn to the west of the Capitol Building. On that same day, March 14, 1965, Mr. Nishikawa (Sang Ik Choi) and Kenji (Daikon) Ohnuki arrived in Washington, D.C., from Japan. Mr. Nishikawa joined the Official Party as they traveled west across the northern half of the country. At that point, the group consisted of Rev. Moon, Mrs. Choi, Miss Kim, and Mr. Nishikawa as well as George Norton and Gordon Ross who drove. Miss Kim described the travel pattern:

> As we traveled, we stopped only for the blessing of ground and sometimes we covered several states, blessing several Holy Grounds in one day. Routinely we slept in motels at night. I bought groceries and made sandwiches for our lunch to save time and money. Missing Korean food, we carried hot bean paste which we ate on pieces of lettuce at lunch time. At night we often went to a Chinese restaurant. Then after driving as far as we could, blessing ground in every state we entered, we slept again. Each day we followed this pattern.[23]

David S.C. Kim joined the party in Salt Lake City and accompanied them through Utah, Idaho, Montana, Washington and Oregon where the final Holy Ground was blessed in Eugene. A local member there described the final ceremony:

> First we made a quick tour of the historic places in Eugene where Miss Kim lived and worked when she was here, then quickly selected a park for the Sacred Ground. The spot selected has five trees all growing out of a common root, with a large stone in front where one can sit. This was the last Sacred Ground to be dedicated during Master's trip. When the ceremony was completed he shouted in English, "Finished!" and strode away from the Sacred Ground as if a great victory had been won.[24]

Arriving back in the Bay Area on March 30, the circuit was complete. At this point, Rev. Moon flew east to celebrate "Parents' Day" with the Washington, D.C., group while Miss Kim stayed on the West Coast to celebrate with the "Western Family." At Rev. Moon's request, she returned to Washington, D.C., shortly afterwards and departed for England on April 26, 1965 with "the assignment of teaching the Principle to the English people."[25] At the same time, Doris Walder left for Italy to become the church's first missionary there. Teddy Verheyen had already departed for Holland. The significance of establishing missions in twelve different nations was stressed.[26]

Rev. Moon's visit to the United States lasted nearly five months until July 1, 1965, when he left for Europe. Besides establishing Holy Grounds, he called a twenty-one day training session in Washington, D.C., continued touring, and spoke frequently. By June, members were ready with the first edition of *The Master Speaks*, seven edited, in-house transcriptions of question and answer sessions with Rev. Moon taped at various centers throughout the country.[27] In addition to activities within the church, Rev. Moon also initiated several contacts outside. Two of these were of particular note: his 'sitting' with well-known American trance-medium, Arthur Ford and his visit with former president, Dwight D. Eisenhower.

Along with Jeanne Dixon, one of the nation's most well known psychics and famous for his sittings with Madame Henri Houdini and later with Bishop James A. Pike, Arthur Ford did a sitting with Rev. Moon in March, 1965. Sir Anthony Brooke had prepared the way for this meeting the previous November. In that session, Ford's communicator, Fletcher, had testified to the Rev. Moon. The same testimony continued in the session with Rev. Moon:

> FLETCHER: It is not easy for me to get down to the level of Ford. Great power in the form of light — if you were to see the light that surrounds you — most of you would be blinded by it. . . .

In another setting I would insist that my instrument and the rest of you should take off your shoes. But spiritually you can create the humility that will enable you to know that you are in the presence of truth—Incarnate and Discarnate. . . .

Sun Myung Moon is the one I have been talking about. I have been speaking for a group of people here. This group seems to surround him. And the power that flows through him, the intelligence, is not just one—it is a great group of people. And they seem all to draw their inspiration and their knowledge from One Source—and then they seem to pour it symbolically into a pool and in some strange symbolical way that pool becomes Sun Myung Moon. . . .

COL. PAK: Could you give me some forecast of our leader's work, the teaching and educational process of this new truth in the United States?

FLETCHER: First of all, he must be willing to listen, to speak, and then have his words translated —and they will be translated into many languages. But you cannot expect the message to be accepted immediately by vast numbers of people—only those who are ready and who are willing to listen and to whom this particular message seems to be right and meaningful. That is the way that all the world teachers have had to go. And remember one thing only, that if it is of God, it cannot fail. And it is of God.

Excerpts from the verbatim record of both "The Sun Myung Moon Sittings" were later incorporated as a chapter in Arthur Ford's *Unknown But Known* (Harper & Row, 1968).[28]

During his stay in Washington, D.C., Rev. Moon also initiated contacts with several political figures to whom he introduced the movement and its objectives and asked for support. By far, the most well-known contact of this kind was former President Dwight D. Eisenhower, whom Rev. Moon met in Gettysburg, Pennsylvania on June 25, 1965. According to the *New Age Frontiers*, the meeting was most successful:

Although we knew that the General was a very busy
man, it was plain that he didn't want us (i.e., Mrs.
Won Pak Choi, Col. Bo Hi Pak, Kenji Ohnuki, and
Gordon Ross, along with Rev. Moon) to leave. In his
private office upstairs, he began to explain the origin
and significance of every gift on display . . . . Finally,
no gifts remained to be explained. Escorting our Leader
to the door, he said that he was honored by this visit
and wished our Leader the greatest success. Our Leader
smiled broadly, thanked him again for the hospitality,
and said goodbye.

Time originally allotted for our Leader's visit—5
minutes. Time spent with General Eisenhower—45
minutes! Truly a successful day![29]

The World Tour

It is difficult to determine the impact Rev. Moon's visit to
America had on the Bay Area church. If one were to judge by
the *New Age Frontiers*, the impact was decisive:

Suffice to say that our Leader left behind him a Family
whose dedication and devotion are now supreme. The
car had no sooner left the driveway in Oakland than the
Bay Area groups swung into action. There is so much
to be done, so many to contact, to teach, to tell this
marvelous true message! If we were convinced before,
our conviction now is absolute. We must work and
grow and accomplish. . . . There is nothing else we can
do, no other way we can go, no other cause so worthy
than returning the world to God, our Father! To this
end, we pledge our blood, sweat and tears![30]

On the other hand, one sees little evidence of new activity. From
February to July, news of Rev. Moon in America dominated the
newsletter. After July 1, 1965, it was dominated by news of his
world tour. However, as a number of members in the Bay Area

had been "furiously engaged" during June "in arranging financing to assist the . . . continuing trip around the world,"[31] they had a stake and involvement in the journey.

After a short trip to Canada and several South American countries, Rev. Moon along with Mrs. Won Pok Choi and Mr. Nishikawa (Sang Ik Choi) began the European portion of the tour, a portion that was marked by meetings with eight previous Bay Area members now missionaries on that continent. In London, Miss Kim, six new contacts and a limousine Anthony Brooke sent met the group at the airport. The following day the group blessed ground at a place "near Peter Pan in Kensington Gardens,"[32] and visited many sites such as Windsor Castle, Eton College (which Anthony Brooke had attended), the Houses of Parliament, Westminster Abbey, St. Paul's Cathedral, the Tower of London, the British Museum, the National Gallery and Buckingham Palace.

Miss Kim rejoined the tour, and they went to Copenhagen, on July 20, 1965. From there, the Official Party traveled to Oslo and Stockholm before arriving at Tempeldorf Airport in West Berlin where Peter Koch and Ursula Schumann, original pioneers in Germany who had left the San Francisco Bay Area sometime before met them.[33] The next day ground was blessed in Berlin. Ursula Schumann described the ceremony:

> The ceremony was set at 6 p.m. in the park near the zoo, opposite from the Pillar of Victory. Our Leader preferred a young tree which will stand for many years to come. Mrs. Choi was taking her position in the North, representing the position of our Leader and our Mother, Mr. Nishikawa was assigned to stand in the East, Peter as representative of the country in the West, and Miss Kim as main missionary in the South. Then I was placed several steps behind Miss Kim. Our Leader offered a prayer, sprinkled salt and soil, and buried the pebble. We were completely drenched and rushed to get to the City Hall of Schoeneberg where all official festivities took place. With an umbrella, our Leader

obtained a fairly large stone, took soil from a
flowerpot, and handed it over to Mrs. Choi.[34]

Rev. Moon and party arrived in Frankfurt Germany, on July
28, 1965, where they met Paul and Christel Werner, their son,
Klaus, Barbara Koch (Peter's sister) and Elke Klawiter, all of
whom had joined in the San Francisco Bay Area. In addition,
there were seven new German members. From Essen, Germany,
the Official Party plus Peter Koch and Paul Werner began their
trip across Europe. First stop was Amsterdam, Holland, where
they met Teddy Verheyen who presented them with the first
Dutch translation of the Principle. From there, the group
proceeded to Belgium, Luxembourg, France, Switzerland,
Austria and Italy where they met Doris Walder.

In the course of the European trip, the group visited a
multitude of historic sites including the Cathedral of Notre Dame
and the Eiffel Tower in Paris, the former League of Nations'
Building as well as Calvin's church in Geneva, and the
Coliseum, catacombs, Circus Maximus and Vatican in Rome.
Again, however, the key purpose was not sight-seeing. A kind
of 'divine compulsion' was well expressed in Peter Koch's
description of a museum in Brussels:

> After blessing Holy Ground in a park opposite the
> King's residence, our Leader wanted to visit a certain
> museum. However, by the time we arrived there it was
> almost closing time. Nevertheless, in order to make a
> condition we had to visit the museum. The whole
> building! In eight minutes! I never laughed so much as
> I did on that occasion. Imagine seven heavenly soldiers
> with smiling faces running through the exhibition halls
> like a storm![35]

Having blessed ground in front of St. Peter's Basilica at the
Vatican, Rev. Moon and party traveled to the more ancient lands
of Greece, Egypt and the Middle East. While remnants of the
Acropolis and pyramids were impressive to the group, the most

poignant stops were in the Holy Land. Arriving in Amman, Jordan, on August 28, 1965, they were met by Major Maduber, a friend who had heard the Principle in Washington, D.C. Together they visited many sites: Mt. Nebo, where Moses looked out over the Promised Land; the Jordan River at the place where Jesus was thought to have been baptized; the Mount of Temptation on which a Greek Orthodox monastery stood; Jericho; the Dead Sea; Mt. Gerizim; Jacob's well; and, finally, Jerusalem: St. Anne's tomb, Pilate's court, the prison where Jesus was kept before his crucifixion, the road he walked to Calvary, Gethsemane, and the Rock of Agony. Miss Kim wrote:

> Each holy place is occupied by one, two or three churches which are built right on the holy place, so one loses sight of the original natural scenes. Yet it is quite touching to visit these places. Our Leader and all of us burst into tears as he prayed on Calvary and Gethsemane.[36]

Rev. Moon set up Holy Grounds on Mt. Nebo, Mt. Gerizim, Gethsemane and at Hebron; then traveled to Syria on September 3, 1965 and blessed ground in the desert outside of Damascus. From there, they traveled to Beirut, Lebanon, where ground was sanctified on the beach facing the Mediterranean. Because of the political situation, they were unable to enter Israel to visit such sites as Mt. Zion, Nazareth, or Galilee.

The unstable political situation in the Middle East was a foretaste of the general instability that marked the rest of the world tour. A cholera epidemic in Iraq prohibited stopping there, and in Tehran, the group learned of the war between Pakistan and India. Avoiding Pakistan entirely, it was only after some difficulty that the party got out of India and traveled to Singapore, Malaya, Thailand (they were refused visas to Burma), and Vietnam which they found "full of Americans, GI's and military trucks." This was their "most unpleasant" stay of the journey as "most of the hotels . . . had been either taken over or reserved by the Americans." Vietnam was followed by Manila,

capital of the Philippines, where Mr. Nishikawa was assaulted by
two youths who tried to steal his wrist watch and camera. The
party arrived in Hong Kong on September 24, 1965; Taipei,
capital of Nationalist China, two days later, and finally Tokyo
where they were received "by an excited crowd of the Japanese
Family" on September 29th. Miss Kim wrote:

> After 12 days of sightseeing and visiting in Tokyo and
> vicinity, on October 10 we put our Leader and Mrs.
> Choi on the plane for Korea. It was exactly 260 days
> since his departure from Korea.[37]

Back to the Bay Area

Miss Kim arrived back in the Bay Area on October 11,
1965. That her arrival was unexpected but welcome was
reflected in Mary Fleming's report in the October issue of *New
Age Frontiers*:

> Miss Kim is back! She arrived yesterday from
> Tokyo and took us all by surprise. The first indication
> we had of her arrival was a telephone call from the
> airport; Miss Kim wanted to know which bus she
> should take to which Center in the Bay Area! Needless
> to say, we broke all records getting to her.[38]

Miss Kim, however, was not the only Korean missionary to
have arrived in the Bay Area. Mr. David S.C. Kim, having
completed a Master's Degree in Psychological Counselling from
the University of Oregon, where he enrolled after being expelled
for 'heresy' from Western Conservative Baptist Seminary just
before his graduation in 1961, came to the Bay Area from the
Northwest the previous June to work on his visa situation. Once
again, the two missionaries were living in close proximity to one
another: Mr. Kim at Edwin Ang's apartment in Berkeley; Miss
Kim at the Martin's in Oakland. Just what their relationship

would be was unclear, although there were two possible indicators in late October: the establishment of a new Holy Ground in Oakland; and the celebration of the 1965 Children's Day at La Honda, California.

The first church Holy Ground in the U.S. set up by anyone other than Rev. Moon, "Oak Heart" Holy Ground was sanctified by Miss Kim on October 17, 1965. Gathering early that morning at "Father's Peak" in San Francisco, the first Holy Ground established by Rev. Moon in America, members gathered rocks and soil and crossed the San Francisco/Oakland Bay Bridge by caravan to Lakeside Park by Lake Merritt in Oakland. There, encircled by "nine majestic Italian Stone Pine trees," the spot chosen was a point of land extending farthest out into the "heart-shaped lake located in the very heart of Oakland." Lowell Martin described the ceremony:

> Miss Kim stood on this spot at 8:30 a.m. and began the ceremony. Jim Fleming stood in the north position, Peter Robinson in the east, Edwin Ang in the west and I in the south. All others present stood in the children's position twelve paces behind the south position. . . .
>
> As we departed from the ceremony to gather at the Oakland Center, someone remarked, "Miss Kim first lived in a Principled home on the Hill of Oaks (with the Pumphreys on Oak Hill in Oregon). Now she has blessed her first Holy Ground in the Land of Oaks (Oakland)."[39]

Although Mr. David Kim had been absent from the Holy Ground ceremony in Oakland, the weekend Children's Day celebration at La Honda, California, October 22-24, 1965, was a coming together not only for Bay Area members but also for members from Oregon and Los Angeles. Alternating talks by Miss Kim and David Kim were followed by a question and answer period, warm fellowship, worship, a brief Board meeting and recreation. There was no hint of disharmony. As one member wrote, "Everything and everybody contributed to an ideal time."[40]

Whether Miss Kim and David Kim could have worked together at this point to reconstruct the Bay Area community was unlikely. In any event, they were not given the chance. Mr. Kim, in order to stay in the country, took a counseling position with the Job Corps which led him to Clearfield, Utah where he coordinated activities of the "Northwest Family" until 1971. Miss Kim soon afterwards relocated in Washington, D.C., where she maintained "national headquarters" until 1972. While the reasons for Mr. Kim's departure were rather clear, the rationale behind Miss Kim's move was more complex. In order to understand her decision to relocate, it is important to note the appearance of yet two more Korean missionaries in the San Francisco Bay Area.

The first of these was Mr. Nishikawa (Sang Ik Choi). Previously deported from Japan in 1964, Mr. Nishikawa knew before joining the world tour that his mission there was over, and Rev. Moon suggested that he pioneer Chicago. A postscript in the November 1965 *New Age Frontiers* announced his arrival in the Bay Area:

> Mr. Nishikawa arrived tonight (Nov. 12 on Pan American Flight 346 from Tokyo. He will stay ln the Bay Area for a short time before proceeding to his new mission field in Eastern United States. Because his passport is in his Korean name, and his travel must necessarily be in that name, he requests that we address him as Sang Ik Choi—Mr. Choi (pronounced Chay as in chair).[41]

The second Korean missionary who appeared in the Bay Area at this time was Col. Bo Hi Pak,who arrived December 3, 1965. On that day, the four earliest Unification Church missionaries to America were gathered in the San Francisco Bay Area: Miss Kim, Mr. Kim, Mr. Choi, and Col. Pak. Although

Col. Pak stayed only one day, he brought news that hastened in Miss Kim's departure. She wrote simply:

> In the end of 1965 I came to Washington, D.C., at the request of Mr. Pak bringing our California corporation papers to establish headquarters in Washington. It had become impossible for Mr. Pak to continue spiritual work because of his career.[42]

While Col. Pak's situation was the immediate cause for Miss Kim's departure, there were two additional reasons why she was willing to relocate: the advantages of Washington; and the limitations of the Bay Area.

There were at least three distinct considerations that could have influenced Miss Kim in her decision to relocate to Washington. First, that was where Rev. Moon stayed during his visit to America. As a result, the center there had gained a good deal of prestige.[43] Not only had the Washington members started referring to their center as headquarters, but being located in the nation's capital, the center appeared to offer more of a focus for nationwide activities. A two-week "MidWinter Training Session" for new members throughout the country was already scheduled to begin there December 20, 1965. Second, in Washington, Miss Kim would be in closer proximity to the European mission, the leaders of which were all from the Bay Area. Third and perhaps primary, by relocating in Washington, D.C., Miss Kim would have the opportunity to solve "the problem of two existing corporations" and to deal with Col. Pak's rival text.[44]

If there were positive reasons for Miss Kim to relocate in Washington, those advantages were reinforced by three distinct drawbacks in the Bay Area. First, there was factionalization. Although relations among centers in Burlingame, San Francisco, Oakland, and Berkeley were cordial, there was little interaction. Second, there was the possibility of rival missionaries, first Mr. Kim and now Mr. Choi. Third, and most important, the community style that had developed in the Bay Area during her absence was different than before. There were children and animals. Members appeared encumbered by family and career responsibilities.

Thus, the decision was made. Sandi and John Pinkerton flew up to the Bay Area from Los Angeles on December 10th for "a last talk with Miss Kim before she left and Sandi started her trip across the country and on to England." The last Sunday service before Miss Kim's departure was held at the Berkeley Center the following day, and on December 12, 1965, members gathered at the airport to see off Miss Kim and Jim Adams, a serviceman who would accompany her as far as Denver.

Equally significant as Miss Kim's decision to go to Washington was Mr. Choi's decision to remain in the Bay Area. This began a new phase in the church's development. Kenji (Daikon) Ohnuki and Yun Soo Lim arrived in the Bay Area from Washington D.C., on December 11, 1965, to be with Mr. Choi. At Miss Kim's Farewell Service, Mr. Choi, Daikon and Soo Lim sang two songs from the Japanese church. By the December 21 they had moved into a new center in San Francisco. On December 28, 1965, Mr. Choi's wife and their 100-day-old son, Jen Ki arrived. Shirley Robinson, living in San Francisco Center #1 wrote poignantly:

> During these last two months it has been as if our Father were saying to us, "Yes, I have had to send away some of those you love, but because of my love for you I send others to you."[45]

A whole new story was ready to unfold in the Bay Area.

NOTES

1. "News from Korea," *New Age Frontiers*, January 15, 1963; April 15, 1963.

2. Young Oon Kim, *Memoirs,* Dec. 1963.

3. Ibid., November 1963.

4. Young Oon Kim, "Our Time Has Come," *New Age Frontiers*, January 1, 1964.

5. Doris Walder, "News from L.A.," *New Age Frontiers*, March 1, 1964. The "Universal Link" groups, in England and the United States during the 1960s were an informal fellowship of like-minded individuals centered upon a number of "channels" who were delivering messages of the cosmic operations ushering in the new age. Much expectancy focussed on December 1967, when there was hope for an objective event, a spectacular change in universal thinking, which would signal the coming new age. See J. Gordon Melton, The Encyclopedia of American Religions, Vol II (Wilmington, N.C.: McGrath, 1978), 121-29.

6. Sir Anthony Brooke, *Revelation for the New Age* (London: Regency Press, 1967), 90-91.

7. Young Oon Kim, "News from Korea," *New Age Frontiers*, March 15 1964; Lofland, *Doomsday Cult*, 260.

8. Bob Oswald, "Testimony from St. Louis," *New Age Frontiers*, July, 1965; Anthony Brooke, "News from England," *New Age Frontiers*, April 15, 1964; "Former Rajah Muda Gives a Talk on 'Toward Human Unity'," *New Age Frontiers*, June 15, 1965.

9. Young Oon Kim, "News from Korea," *New Age Frontiers*, June 1, 1964.

10. Young Oon Kim, "News from Korea," *New Age Frontiers*, October 1 1964.

11. John Pinkerton, "News from Sacramento," *New Age Frontiers*, March 1, 1964.

12. Jim Fleming, "News from San Francisco," *New Age Frontiers*, March 15, 1964.

13. See Regis Hanna, "Report on the National Director's Conference," *New Age Frontiers*, January 1971.

14. See *New Age Frontiers*, March 1964-December 1965.

15. Jim and Mary Fleming, "News from Burlingame," *New Age Frontiers*, November 1, 1964; "News from St. Louis," *New Age Frontiers*, December 15, 1964.

16. Mary Fleming, "Report from Burlingame," *New Age Frontiers*, September 1965.

17. They included Pearl World, Lovie Smith, Esther Samematsu, Yvonne Owens and Hildegard Kress. See "News from Berkeley," *New Age Frontiers*, June 1965.

18. "High Noon Prayer Vigil," *New Age Frontiers*, September 1, 1964.

19. Kim, *"Memoirs,"* 1965.

20. "Hail to the Brightness," *New Age Frontiers*, February 15, 1965.

21. Ibid.

22. "List of Holy Places in the United States with Description of their Location," *New Age Frontiers*, May 15, 1965.

23. Kim, *"Memoirs,"* 1965.

24. David Bridges, "The Master's Northern Visits: Eugene, Oregon," *New Age Frontiers*, May 15, 1965.

25. Kim, *"Memoirs,"* December 1963.

26. Gordon Ross, "The Significance of the Passover Ceremony," *New Age Frontiers*, June 15, 1965.

27. "The Master Speaks," *New Age Frontiers*, June 15, 1965.

28. Arthur Ford, "The Sun Myung Moon Sittings," *Unknown But Known* (New York: Harper & Row, 1968), 114-123.

29. Gordon Ross, "Eisenhower Meets Our Leader," *New Age Frontiers*, July 15, 1965.

30. "Hail to the Brightness," *New Age Frontiers*, February 15, 1965.

31. Jim Fleming, "Report from Burlingame," *New Age Frontiers*, June 1, 1965.

32. Young Oon Kim, "Europe's Blessing: London to Stockholm," *New Age Frontiers*, August 1965.

33. Kim, *"Memoirs,"* May, 1963.

34. Ursula Schumann, "Europe's Blessing: Berlin, Germany," *New Age Frontiers*, August 1965.

35. Peter Koch, "Eurasian Glory: Germany to Italy," *New Age Frontiers*, September 1965.

36. Young Oon Kim, "Toward the East and Toward the Glorious Land—Visit to the Holy Land," *New Age Frontiers*, October 1965.

37. "Saigon to Korea." *New Age Frontiers*, October 1965.

38. Mary Fleming, "Report from Burlingame," *New Age Frontiers*, October 1965.

39. Lowell Martin, "Oak Heart: A New Holy Ground," *New Age Frontiers*, November 1965.

40. Shirley Robinson, "Report from San Francisco," *New Age Frontiers*, November 1965.

41. "Postscript," *New Age Frontiers*, November 1965.

42. Kim, *"Memoirs,"* 1965.

43. "Reports from Washington, D.C., *New Age Frontiers*, July-December, 1965.

44. Kim, *"Memoirs,"* 1965.

45. Shirley Robinson, "News from San Francisco," *New Age Frontiers*, January 1966.

CHAPTER FOUR

THE RE-EDUCATION FOUNDATION: 1966–71

Mr. Choi Joins the Movement—The Mission to Japan— Early Days in San Francisco—The Re-Education Center International Exchange Press—The Principles of Education—Founding the International Ideal City—The International Re-Education Foundation—Friendship Banquets—The Pioneer Academy—Final Success

If the middle 1960s were years of transition for the Unification Church in the Bay Area, the late 1960s were years of transformation. This transformation was reflected, most fundamentally, in a radically different membership profile and approach. Whereas members previously had been older, often married and relatively established, the accent in the late 1960s was on youth. Members who joined during this period were, for the most part, in their early twenties, unmarried and unattached. At the same time, whereas previously the church had been concerned with proclaiming its message, the accent in the late 1960s was on action. "Salvation," as one piece of church literature put it, "is not to speak about [the] heavenly kingdom but to actualize it."[1]

Given the focus on youth and action, the thrust of the church in the late 1960s was less theological than educational and finally utopian. The concern was both for instruction and for the establishment of institutions reflecting utopian ideals. Rather than through spiritualists or prophecy, hope and excitement were generated through a consummate effort to set up an "International Ideal City." Three key factors contributed to this development: a new church community, changes in the San Francisco Bay Area environment and the figure of Sang Ik Choi.

A new church community. The story of the Unification Church in the Bay Area during the late 1960s had its beginnings, no less than during the early 1960s, in a transplanted community of believers. Rather than from Oregon, however, this community came from Japan. In this sense, one key factor contributing to developments in the Bay Area community was the pattern of life established in the Japanese church.

Changes in the Bay Area environment. If the new church community was from an entirely different locale, the Bay Area to which it came also was markedly different. On the one hand, institutional breakdown resulting from assassinations, campus protest, racial confrontations and draft resistance had produced the first supply of disaffected youth. On the other hand, idealism implicit in the Haight-Ashbury hippie district had cast a utopian tint over the entire Bay Area.

The figure of Sang Ik Choi. While the interplay between the new church community and changes in the Bay Area environment helped produce the transformation referred to at the beginning of this section, of more import was the figure of Sang Ik Choi. No less than Miss Kim for her group, Mr. Choi shaped the character of the local church. In this sense, the story of the Unification Church in the Bay Area during this period begins with his story.

Mr. Choi Joins the Movement

Unfortunately, the printed sources relating to Mr. Choi's life before the Unification Church are limited to a transcribed talk delivered by Michiko Matsumoto, the first disciple of the Japanese church. Entitled, "The Road Rev. Nishikawa

Followed," the full transcription amounts to only ten pages.[2] Nonetheless, it includes relevant biographical detail that, as in the case of Miss Kim, can be grouped under the headings of formative influences, conversion and mission.

Formative influences

The most obvious formative influence in Mr. Choi's early life was his upbringing in Japan. Raised at Namba, Osaka, from age two through his college years, Mr. Choi returned to Korea only after the second World War. At that time, many Koreans living in Japan, including Mr. Choi's family, were forced to return. Although he could speak both Japanese and English (he got a job interpreting for occupying G.I. forces), it wasn't until then that Mr. Choi began to learn Korean.

The second formative influence for Mr. Choi was his father's involvement with Tenri-kyo, one of the new religions of Japan and Korea.[3] First as a devoted disciple and later as chief of a local church, Mr. Choi's father began to see himself in different terms after returning to Korea. Mrs. Matsumoto noted:

> One day when his father became sick with a high fever, he began to say something unusual, "I am a King." The family, who gathered around him were so surprised ... he acted as if he were a real king, and his family thought he was . . . mad. But in order to make himself a true missionary of Tenri-kyo, he exhausted all his fortune for religious things: He built a shrine. During its construction, workers were obligated to wear white clothing and to work without smoking and drinking. And they prayed to the sun. . . . His father's sister sympathized with him and made a king's garment for him, in which he walked around with dignity.[4]

Because the family became poor as a result of his father's activity, Mr. Choi, as eldest son, was forced to support them. As a result, he reacted against religion. As Mrs. Matsumoto noted,

He loved liquor very much and drank twice as much as
others did. . . . Because I had known him only as a
devoted disciple, I was surprised to hear that he was a
real alcoholic. . . . He spent all his money for alcohol
and the people. The last thing he cared for was
religion. He didn't believe in God and was afraid of
behaving like his father.

Conversion

A turning point in Mr. Choi's life came when he was
persuaded to attend a week-long Christian revival meeting on the
side of a mountain. A woman dentist friend had promised a
pentecost experience. According to Mrs. Matsumoto, "Rev.
Nishikawa was curious and decided to follow her as if they were
going on a picnic." However, it was at this revival, that Mr.
Choi converted to Christianity. Mrs. Matsumoto described his
experience:

While everyone was praying seriously, Rev. Nishikawa
was in an unobserved corner; he hesitated to pray. He
had never prayed before and did not know how. But
since he was obliged to pray, he did. His first words to
God were "How are you God?" After that he was not
what he had been. He was crying and praying for
repentance with incredible words, "The universe is
dirty. Human beings are dirty. Please pass judgment on
me strictly. Destroy such an impure world." He tore a
jacket, hit his breast with his hands, and threw a rock
into the sea. And the sky turned red, and he heard a
voice, "Who can save this impure world?" He
answered, "I will. Please judge me." The voice said, "I
love thee." "How can I answer you, God? I will present
you this watch given by my friend," and he threw the
watch away. Watching this, everyone around him was
so surprised and shocked.[5]

Mission

Having become a Christian, Mr. Choi smuggled himself from Korea into Japan (the two countries had not restored diplomatic relations) and entered a holiness theological school. On graduating, he returned to Korea during the Korean War and became a war clergyman. After the war, he worked as an interpreter for the U.S. Army, helped distribute food to war orphans, and started an independent holiness church. In 1957, he heard of the Unification Church but was skeptical. Mrs. Matsumoto noted:

> There were a lot of religions in Korea. Everybody knew the end was approaching. He came across the name of the Unification Church. He thought this was an imitation. God is the only one who can unify the world, nevertheless, man was doing. How arrogant they were. He even prayed for God to forgive their arrogance.[6]

One day, however, in April, 1957, Mr. Choi met a friend who went to the Unification Church and who persuaded him to attend a lecture. Although Mr. Choi was to be engaged in three days, he agreed. Again, Mrs. Matsumoto set the scene:

> When about ten persons gathered for a lecture in a room with a blackboard in Seoul, a little woman entered the room and said, "Let's pray before hearing God's words." Rev. Nishikawa thought she fooled him. But once he listened to her pray, he was [so] amazed [as] to cry. The regular prayer always says, "Give me . . . Forgive me. . . ." But hers was different. She prayed to comfort God . . . he listened to her lecture for the whole three days, and he leaned toward her theory.
> He got excited. . . . and asked his fiancee to hear this, but she refused. So he ended that relationship.[7]

Mr. Choi also ended his relationship with the holiness Church. Quitting his ministry, he joined the Unification Church. He went on a forty-day mission to the Korean countryside during the summer and founded a church. More important were the sentiments he expressed a year later:

> When I think of myself a year ago, before I had heard the Principles, and when, in April, I heard them and was deeply impressed, I immediately thought, "I would like to bring these words to Japan."[8]

The Mission to Japan

Sang Ik Choi was the Unification Church's missionary to Japan from 1958 until 1964. The pattern of church life that emerged in Japan during that period was the result of three interrelated factors: the leadership of Mr. Choi, the national ethos of Japan, and the contingencies of the time. As it was this Japanese pattern of church life that was 'exported' to the Bay Area in the late 1960s, it is worthwhile to consider each of these factors individually.

The leadership of Mr. Choi

No less than Miss Kim in America, Mr. Choi had relative autonomy in developing the Japanese movement. Reverend Moon offered him no instructions or suggestions. The situation is nicely illustrated in Michiko Matsumoto's description of Mr. Choi's 'commission':

> He told the great leader [Rev. Moon], through President Eu, that he would like to go to Japan for mission. The great leader answered, "Do as you like." When he left . . . he went to the great leader who was praying deep in the mountains. He just said, "Good luck!" and did not even pray for him or order him.

> Why? Before Rev. Nishikawa, three missionaries went
> to Japan, but they failed because of persecution,
> temptation, hunger, and so on. It was just at the time
> when the great leader was thinking of sending
> somebody to Japan that Rev. Nishikawa said by himself
> that he would go. The great leader wanted to celebrate,
> encourage, and order something for Rev. Nishikawa.
> But . . . he thought it was better to admire him after he
> succeeded. He only prayed, "I wish he could do as he
> likes."[9]

Mr. Choi made known his desire to undertake the mission to
Japan on May 27, 1958. Speaking to Mr. Eu on the second floor
of the Pusan church, he kept his plans secret from everyone else.
One reason for secrecy was that Mr. Choi had decided, once
again, to stowaway. Having met with the captain of the trading
ship *Kinsekikon* in a Pusan coffee shop, Mr. Choi anticipated an
early June departure.

Following a trip to Seoul and his meeting with Rev. Moon
in the mountains near Taegu, Mr. Choi returned to Pusan in
"high spirits." Nonetheless, beginning in Pusan, he confronted
a number of obstacles. First, the captain had not made the agreed
upon arrangements. Second, the ship was delayed. Third, a
disturbing message came from Seoul. Mr. Choi wrote:

> A telegram came from Seoul ordering me to return
> there. "Stop," it said. I wanted to die. After having
> sworn to go, and departed, how could I return to
> Seoul? It would be better to die. I sent a letter and a
> telegram asking them to wait three more days, and I
> hurried up my departure. The command was from
> Master, how could I disobey it? But I had resolved to
> go and departed; I could not return. . . . No matter
> what, I vowed to go, and I am determined. Even if I
> die in fulfilling my vow, I must go because I believe
> that I am going to save the Japanese and all of the
> peoples of the world.[10]

Although doing "as he liked," Mr. Choi may have had occasion to wish he had returned to Seoul. Not only was his money stolen by shipmates (who used it to buy seaweed which they sold and split the profits), but also he, the captain, crew, and ship were seized by Japanese port authorities near Hiroshima on June 21, 1958. Forced to endure a six-month jail sentence, Mr. Choi only avoided compulsory repatriation at his release by fasting to induce illness. Escaping from a sanatorium where he was sent, he made his way to Tokyo. Still, his problems were not over. According to Mrs. Matsumoto,

> Nobody listened to him. He was always refused. He had no money, no food, no clothes, and was so exhausted as to cough out blood from tuberculosis from which he had suffered in his youth. But he went on mission. He slept in parks or playgrounds of schools fearing to be in the crowds. When he looked at himself on the glass window, he was shocked to see such a miserable figure . . . with long hair, a pale face, and a skinny body.[11]

For six months after escaping the sanatorium there was no progress. Finally, he got a job "as a salesman for a watch shop, 'Ondori-Sha,' at Takadanobaba in Tokyo." During the morning, he worked; during the afternoon, he proselytized. Once a week, he rented the second floor of the shop to preach. Yet, as he noted, "Not many came." Still, he wanted to start a church and printed pamphlets with the name, "World Christ Unification Divine Spiritual Association." According to his missionary diary, the founding of the Japanese "Unification Church Association" took place Friday, October 12, 1959. Mr. Choi, however, was the only real member. As he noted,

> People came to listen, but I was sad that there were few ardent believers. I had started my missionary work about ten months before and had no genuine results.[12]

This situation continued until Mr. Choi met Michiko Matsumoto in April, 1960. A Korean Christian whose Japanese husband had died of paratyphoid fever during the second World War, Mrs. Matsumoto became a devoted disciple and brought Setsuko, a university student. From that point, the movement began to grow. Following a breakthrough in late 1962 when fifty young leaders of Risshokoseikai converted, the growth was more dynamic.[13] Mr. Choi continued to lead the church in Japan until he was taken by the Immigration Service and deported in 1964.

The national ethos of Japan

The national ethos of Japan was a second important factor in shaping the pattern of church life exported to the Bay Area in the late 1960s. Although loyalty amid adversity, perseverance, and the all-or-nothing quality of Mr. Choi's personal course was influential on members who consciously sought to emulate his samurai pattern, of more import for future Bay Area developments was the Japanese affinity for organization. A tight organizational structure quickly characterized the pattern of church life in Japan. This emphasis was reflected in three important developments: a communal lifestyle, a corporate church structure, and a systematic elaboration of the training session. Although aspects were modified, the Bay Area environment in the late 1960s was receptive to each of these innovations.

A communal lifestyle. Whereas communal living was secondary and a pragmatic necessity among Miss Kim's group in America, it was the basic pattern of church life in Japan from the beginning. Mr. Choi later remarked:

> Actually living together, that system started from Japan. I started it. Even in Korea, they are not living together. But in Japan . . . I thought we needed a strong movement of dedicated people living together . . . so I started living together in Japan.[14]

Living together also implied working together. From the beginning, rather than holding separate jobs as in America, the Japanese movement sought common employment: first in "haihin kaishu," the door-to-door collection of newspapers, magazines, bottles, and old clothing to be resold to junk dealers; and later, in small church-run businesses.[15]

A corporate church structure. The cooperation and communication that facilitated living and working together was also reflected in a tighter church organization. Rather than a loose association as in America, the church in Japan took on more of the qualities of a corporation. The island was divided into 11 districts which, in turn, were divided into prefectural churches (there were 36 of these by 1966). At the same time, there was a strong national headquarters in Tokyo. Not only were the strongest members transferred from the districts to headquarters, but headquarters, itself, was highly organized into bureaus, departments, divisions and committees. A 1966 report asserted, "with such a center, the local churches can be united and revitalized. And from this center, Japan can be united with the world."[16]

A systematic training program. The organizational emphasis that characterized lifestyle and church structure in Japan was also reflected in a systematic training program. As contrasted with the more haphazard development in America, the training session in Japan achieved a significantly higher level of sophistication. Varying in length from three to forty days and either "on an introductory level or for study in depth and leadership training," there was a separate training facility and a regular staff. Again, as contrasted with the informal, almost folksy atmosphere in America, the sessions themselves were far more focused. According to a 1966 report,

> The schedule is characterized by intensive group activity. Trainees meet regularly in groups of eight to ten, to eat, to pray, and to discuss questions and difficulties; they are under the direction of a leader at all times. After the trainees bed down, the leaders gather for

evaluation and planning. They watch the trainees carefully for qualities of leadership, for participation, and for any problems that might arise.[17]

Contingencies of the time

Aside from Mr. Choi's leadership and the organizational emphasis of the culture, the contingencies of the time were a third factor helping to shape the pattern of church life exported to the Bay Area in the late 1960s. The key elements here were the relationship between Korea and Japan, the position of students in Japanese life, and the era of post-war reconstruction in Japan.

Korea and Japan. While Miss Kim gained access and garnered interest among certain groups in America because of her Korean origins, Mr. Choi's experience in Japan was quite the opposite. Because of long-standing conflicts, the most recent being Japan's occupation of Korea (1905-1945), there were bitter and prejudicial feelings on both sides. Not until 1965 did the two nations establish diplomatic relations, and even then the action was marred by protest.[18]

This situation forced Mr. Choi to become a stowaway and change his name to missionize Japan. More important, it affected his presentation of the Principle. If Miss Kim labored under the fact of a new revelation, Mr. Choi labored under the point of its origin. There was no way he could say that the revelation came from Korea or that the new teacher was a Korean. On the other hand, the fact of a new revelation was no problem. Literally hundreds of groups in post-war Japan were proclaiming new revelations. For this reason, the practice in Japan was to focus on the teaching and goals of the group rather than its origin. This emphasis continued in the Bay Area.

Students in Japanese life. From its beginnings, the Japanese movement focused its recruiting efforts on both high school and college students. The results were good. Miss Kim, on her way to Korea in 1964, reported that thirty full-time evangelists were living at Tokyo headquarters, many of whom were "high school boys and girls." At Nagoya, 200 high school students reportedly had become affiliated by 1966. Nor were college students far behind. According to a 1966 article, the "National Student Movement," later known as the Collegiate Association for the Research of Principles (CARP), comprised "approximately 350 active members in 60 universities throughout Japan."[19] Although not all CARP members were church members, those who were made up a substantial portion of the movement.

There were two important reasons why the Japanese church became student-focused. First, jobs were not easy to quit or to find in Japan. Moreover, unlike in America, employment implied a lifetime commitment. Hence, the employed were less accessible. Second, students in post-war Japan had a good deal of prestige and were influential in the larger society. As a consequence, the movement concentrated its efforts on students through witnessing, through display tables, and, most effectively, through organizing as a club activity on campus. Whereas on American campuses, fraternities and sororities were a focus of student involvement, on Japanese campuses, clubs were at the center of student life. According to one account,

> Each Autumn, all the Japanese universities hold festivals of up to a week in length, at which every club puts up a display. No club had the magnetic power of the Principle Study Group. Outdoors, we street preached and passed out leaflets advertising the display and a forthcoming meeting at which national leaders of the Unification Church and members from that university's club would make introductory speeches on the Principle. Youth and student members from all parts of Tokyo would join to assist wherever a festival was being held.[20]

Post-war reconstruction. One of the biggest boons to the Unification Church as well as to other new religious movements in Japan following the second World War was the era of post-war reconstruction. Whereas Korea was still poor and the

United States had already arrived, Japan was bustling with the excitement of economic expansion. The impact of this expansion upon religion was great. Rather than otherworldly expectations, groups tied into the reconstruction fervor. The Unification Church was no exception.

Mr. Choi was particularly imaginative in his view of the future world. As Michiko Matsumoto noted,

> We enjoyed his theory of "the end." He filled us with a lot of hopes. An apple became as large as a watermelon. On going to the neighborhood, we could go there by escalator.[21]

"The end," of course, was really only the beginning. Mr. Choi always emphasized concrete hope. Rather than simply imagining, he would have members draw pictures of homes they would occupy in the ideal world. They would build a city! As skilled as Miss Kim was in generating hope through spiritual prophecy, Mr. Choi was equally adept in generating hope through utopian ideals.

Nor were these just pipe dreams. They were actually building. They had an organization. They had started businesses. Why couldn't the kingdom start from there? Although of a different sort than Miss Kim's, it was this vision that finally integrated the pattern of church life in Japan. It was where the leadership of Mr. Choi, the national ethos of Japan, and the contingencies of the time all came together. More than anything else, it was this vision that was exported to the Bay Area in the late 1960s.

Early Days in San Francisco

The story of the Unification Church and its new beginning in San Francisco during the late 1960s was, again, not the story of a single missionary's endeavor. It was the story of a transplanted community of believers. Rather than moving several hundred miles down the coastline, as happened when the original community began in California, this community transplanted itself from an entirely different culture. The struggle of the community to overcome barriers of culture, to win its first converts, and to establish itself in San Francisco was the earliest portion of their story.

When Mr. Choi arrived in the Bay Area on November 12, 1965, following Rev. Moon's first world tour, Daikon and Soo Lim had already been in Washington, D.C., for several months. As one later report put it, "they were thriving bush-league Americans."[22] Coming to the Bay Area to be with Mr. Choi, the three moved into an apartment at 43rd and Fulton St., San Francisco. Mrs. Choi and Mr. Choi's infant son, Chinki, arrived from Tokyo on December 28th. Then, on February 28, 1966, Enchon Endo, Koro Ishiguro, and Mitsuko Yoshida arrived via boat from Japan. These eight people were the new beginning of the Unification Church in San Francisco during the late 1960s. Everyone lived at the 43rd Street center.

There were several parallels between the new community and Miss Kim's group which had arrived in San Francisco six years previously. Both were transplanted communities, both lived communally, and both struggled to root themselves in the new environment. At the same time, there were significant differences. Aside from disparate points of origin, these differences were reflected, most basically, in a radically different membership profile and approach.

The members whom Miss Kim gathered in the Bay Area in 1960 were, quite simply, all she had. They were the survivors of her Oregon mission. More importantly, they had been with the Principle only a matter of months. The members whom Mr. Choi gathered in the Bay Area in 1966, on the other hand, were a select group. Daikon and Soo Lim had won the right to come to America by being the most effective witnessers in Japan. Mrs. Choi was among the earliest Korean members of the church. Enchon, from Tokyo, was president of the church's High School Students' Association for the Research of Principles (HARP) and among the group of converts from Risshoroseikai. Koro, from Nagoya, was vice-president of the high school association there and among a group of converts from a local Shinto sect.[23] Both were hand-picked by Mr. Choi. Mitsuko Yoshida was national advisor to the high school association. In short, Mr. Choi assembled an elite corps of missionaries: all members for several years, all dedicated, and all successful.

In addition, except for Mr. Choi who was deported, there was less of a sense of desperation in the new community than there had been in Miss Kim's group's headlong flight from Oakhill. Whereas Miss Kim's group had cut all ties with the Northwest and were on their own, Mr. Choi's group still had connections with Japan. This connection meant that there was initial financial support and the possibility of reinforcements. Rather than the uncertainty and tentativeness that had characterized Miss Kim's group, the new group had the assurance and stability of a pattern of church life developed over several years in Japan. As a consequence, there was less trial and error than in Miss Kim's group. Notably, there were no initial attempts at mass conversion through speaking engagements or communication media. This may have been due in part to the language barrier, but, more likely, it was due to a more developed sense of strategy and tactics.

On the other hand, there was no church visitation or serious theological focus as in Miss Kim's group. This was due partly to the fact that most of the members were non-Christian converts and partly to the pattern of church life developed in Japan, where there were few Christian churches. The emphasis, rather, was on action. Members witnessed actively on the streets, in parks, and on campuses. Though avoiding churches, the feeling was much more that of a planned missionary assault.

However, whatever advantages the new group had in membership or approach were offset by the cultural barriers. Having begun activities in March, 1966, the work was difficult. According to a later report,

The next year was probably one of the biggest challenges of their lives. They were literally fired up with
spirit and drive, but the barriers, language, custom, etc.
were almost equal to this drive. Their effort to share
with others was very trying.[24]

For several months, there was no result. Then, during the
summer of 1966, Koro met David Doerring, an Iowa farmboy
who had just arrived in the Bay Area. As the first American to
join the group, his account is revealing:

I was in a tee-shirt part way stretched out on a beach,
looking at the sun, and wondering how I got there.
Koro showed me an address and said, "You come!" I
came and immediately found myself in the world of
oriental custom and tradition. I liked the people, and
when Koro asked me I moved in. . . . [25]

The group continued to work hard. David Doerring noted,
"Competition was a key word, and in an average day Soo and
Daikon would gather the names of thirty or so people." Yet few
responded. Late in 1966, Daikon and Soo Lim met Phyllis
Yamoto, a Japanese-American student at San Francisco State
University. Then, in the spring of 1967, Taco Serizawa (having
come from Japan to take the place of Mitsuko Yoshida who was
ill) met Ron Pepper. According to David Doerring, it was with
Ron that Mr. Choi "could really set his movement into motion":

He was willing to do anything asked of him. He took
the initiative of street speaking in Golden Gate Park
after inspiration from Enchon and Koro and a push
from Daikon.[26]

Soon after Ron Pepper joined, Soo Lim met David Hose, an
aspiring young artist living on the fringe of the Haight-Ashbury
district. Then, in the autumn and early winter came Steve
Mudgett, Clint Steery, Diana Swank and Carmela Acohido.

Although struggles continued, by the end of 1967, the original community of eight had doubled itself with eight new American members. A pattern of doubling membership annually continued until 1971.

While the barriers of language and culture had inhibited the community's early proselytization efforts, it had one other important effect. It hindered communication with other Unification Church members in the Bay Area. Known as the "Japanese Family," Mr. Choi's group went their own way. This was dramatized in June, 1967 when the group incorporated as the International Unification Church—a *separate* incorporation from Miss Kim's Holy Spirit Association for the Unification of World Christianity (HSA-UWC).

The Re-Education Center

Besides differences in the origin and makeup of the two founding communities, there were several differences in their development. While these differences can be expressed in a variety of ways, most fundamental was Mr Choi's decision to create a social movement rather than a church. A split between spiritual and organizational leadership had signaled the demise of Miss Kim's community in the Bay Area. However, a synthesis fashioned between these two kinds of authority led to the growth and development of Mr. Choi's group. Although there are other ways to tell the story of the Re-Education Center, one significant way is in terms of the constructive use made of the tension between spiritual and organizational authority.

The lines of spiritual authority in Mr. Choi's community were grounded in the origin and makeup of the founding group. As in Japan, the community style was communal. While this was a secondary development in Miss Kim's group, it was the primary pattern of Mr. Choi's group from the beginning. Second, the membership in Mr. Choi's original group had sharp disparities in age. This had not been the case in Miss Kim's group. Mr. Choi, however, brought over younger people. The combination of these two factors—a communal lifestyle and sharp disparities of age (virtually alternate generations)—resulted in a pattern of community life resembling that of an extended family. As the community's first newsletter put it,

> Until now, the Center has been referred to as a group or a community, but actually the feeling that is shared is one of a family. In fact, our members relate to each other as brother and sister.[27]

Although Miss Kim's group referred to themselves as a family, the lack of a strongly communal lifestyle and sharp disparities of age made for peer-relationships than the more defined lines of authority characteristic of a family. This situation was apparent in the relative positions of Miss Kim and Mr. Choi. Whereas in print, Miss Kim might be referred to as "our beloved elder sister" or even "our Mother in faith," she was always "Miss Kim" in person. For Mr. Choi, the situation was reversed. In print, he was usually referred to as "Mr. Choi," teacher or educator, while he was always "Papa" in person. As he noted,

> In the beginning nobody called me Mr. Choi. They called me papa; we lived like a family. Now many people call me papasan, but people who lived with me don't call me Mr. Choi or papasan, just papa.[28]

Nor was this a single-parent family as Miss Kim's group had been. Since Mrs. Choi was there, the group also had a 'mamasan'. Along with Mr. Choi's sermons and lectures, community newsletters also devoted space to question and answer sessions with Mrs. Choi. One of the group's student members described the set-up in a term paper:

> The structure of our family stands with Papasan and Mamasan (Mrs. Choi) as the heads of our family. Papa is involved with the educational movement part of

our family. He is continually thinking what is the best way to publicize our Principle to the American people; how he can best teach the brothers in our family to speak and lecture well; how he can influence prominent people in San Francisco. Mamasan works from the other end, internally rather than externally. She involves herself with family members' problems in their family relationships, in the understanding of themselves and then the overcoming of their own weak or negative points such as impatience, arrogance, and insensitivity. Papasan works with the collective family as a revolutionary educational group. Mama works with each individual brother or sister with his or her personal problem. Papa is a great extrovert, always thinking big things, like establishing a Principle university. Mama is an introvert, thinking about her development of character and how to overcome some trait within her. So they are like the yin-yang symbol, complete opposites but extremely complementary.[29]

If the lines of spiritual authority in Mr. Choi's group were relatively set, the lines of organizational authority were subject to the shifting ground of circumstance. Operating in a time and locale of radical questioning, experimentation, and seculariza-tion, the community, as noted, developed an organizational structure that was less churchly and more educational, consciously adapted to an urban environment and newer American members. Mr. Choi was "advisor" to the organization from the beginning and, as in the Japanese church, sought to delegate responsibility.

A combination of these factors produced a pattern of organizational authority that was both flexible and capable of sophistication. The consciousness of being an educational foundation came early. As Mr. Choi noted,

I started as a Unification Church missionary when I came here. Then we started church activities, and I got a little problem. First thing, in San Francisco, people are very liberal. They are not interested in Christianity. In the Orient, Christianity comes from Europe, the West side, civilized country, so right after the second world war was over, they were very interested in Western culture and religion, so I could start it in Japan very easily. After I came to America I was surprised that . . . especially young people in San Francisco were not very much interested in religion . . . and then people who are interested in religion do not want to change anything . . . . Then, at the same time, the hippie movement started. When I saw the hippie people I really hurt. Young men with long hair without any discipline or training, character education. They want to live whatever they want; they have license; they want an easy life. So I thought I better contribute my life to the character education of life rather than religious life. Then this way I can help American society and this way I can be successful rather than by a religious approach.[30]

Thus, the transformation began. Rather than "Divine" Principle, the teaching or ideology (not revelation) was the "Unification" Principle. Rather than on a new society, emphasis was placed on a better society. Rather than the Kingdom of God, the vision was the ideal world, a humanistically inspired utopia constructed along the lines of a comprehensive, universally applicable educational program and principles.

In brief, the organizational structure of the Bay Area group in the late 1960s was more that of a social movement and efforts were made to incorporate a broad base of membership. Although theological sophistication was lost, there were some organizational gains. First, there was a clear-cut distinction between spiritual and organizational authority. Whereas a church structure might blur the distinctions, there was less chance of this with an educational foundation. Hence, Mr. Choi's spiritual authority was not challenged. Second, the educational format afforded American members an outlet for expression and an opportunity to help shape and direct organizational activities. Whereas, in Miss Kim's group, an excessive amount of sophistication might have interfered with spiritual goals, in Mr. Choi's group, excessive sophistication was an eagerly sought-after commodity.

For the Unification Church during the late 1960s in San Francisco, Re-Education was the answer. Mr. Choi combined the attributes of family and organization in a way that made for both stability and growth. By early 1970, the group had three centers in San Francisco as well as satellite centers in San Jose and Palo Alto. Interestingly, emergent patterns were reminiscent of the Japanese church. Although couched in American idiom, the Japanese pattern of church life was reflected clearly in the establishment of a student movement, in group training sessions, and in the public meeting.

Student movement

When the Re-Education Center members purchased their second house at 2065 Sacramento Street, San Francisco, in July, 1969, the previous center at 762 Eighth Avenue became the "Student Center." Sixteen full-time students lived there. While this development paralleled the pattern in Japan, the means of involving students was different. Rather than organizing as a club activity on campus, the Re-Education Center offered "Experimental College" classes. The opportunity for this was part of the radical experimentation in education on many college campuses in the United States during the 1960s. That Mr. Choi's group was able to adapt successfully to this opportunity indicated both organizational flexibility and a degree of sophistication. Classes on the "Dialectical Unification Principle" were weekly offerings on several area campuses. The response was good. At City College of San Francisco, the group's class was filmed as the most successful Experimental College course.[31]

Campus unrest, strife and strikes in 1968 led to the development of the student movement. As previous student leaders were involved in protest activities, the "Unified Students" (members of the Re-Education Center) were able to obtain vacant leadership positions in student government. Steve Hart became Student Body President and David Endo, Student Body Vice-President at City College of San Francisco. Stefan Phaender was appointed Director of Communications on the Student Council at San Francisco State University. Although these were lame-duck positions with small budgets and less interest, success bred hope. An October 1968 "Prospectus for the Establishment of the Student Unification Movement" outlined ambitious plans for a number of projects and the establishment of publications, cultural, recreational and business departments.[32]

Training session

The group's first training session was held in the Palo Alto hills, July 4-7, 1968. Just as with Miss Kim's group, the training session was recognized as a potent device. As Ron Pepper put it following the completion of the first session,

> Although I have explained the Unification Principle many times, I hadn't grasped the deep heart of it until now. We were actually studying the original way of human life and living it during our training period. [33]

While the group's first session had been for resident members, a second weekend session over Labor Day, 1968, included guests. The results were duly noted:

> The Re-Education members and their weekend visitors slept together, ate together, worked together, studied together and lived together. The impact of three short days on each participant was very great. The moments after the last lecture were filled with hand shaking, bear hugging, tears, and broad smiles. How grateful and

> overjoyed were those hearts to have actually heard and
> experienced the truth: Man CAN live in harmony
> exhibiting the beauty of true human feelings and
> character. . . .[34]

Quickly, the training session became the group's chief means
of promoting conversion. As one member stated "If there is no
permanent change in character, then the training session is little
more than an interesting gathering of people."[35]

Again, in developing the training session, the group
demonstrated both adaptability and sophistication. Not only were
the early sessions coordinated to fall on long holiday
weekends—the Fourth of July, Labor Day, Thanksgiving, New
Year's, Easter, Mother's Day—but they became highly
structured. The level of sophistication in the Japanese church was
reflected in the way procedures were routinized. Members
developed elaborate training session manuals and followed
exacting time schedules—for wake-up, exercises, meals, group
meetings, sports, and lectures. Staff responsibilities proliferated
into a number of role functions: Director, Assistant Director,
Lecturers, Exercise Coordinator, Music Makers, Food
Preparation, Registration, Housekeeper, Photographer, and
Recorder.[36]

Public meetings

The Re-Education Center also began to develop activities that
were explicitly cultural. These began as early as November,
1968, with the renovation of the center basement at 762 Eighth
Avenue, the construction of a "Universal Stage," and the first
"Unified Family Production." Soon Ron Pepper was head of the
Cultural Department. Later Clint Steery became music director
and head of the "New Age Band." All of these developments
were utilized in the center's most ambitious project to date: the
Public Meeting.

Held at the Unitarian Center in San Francisco, these
meetings were monthly affairs between October and March,

1969-70. They featured entertainment, expositions of the center's activities, and speeches by Mr. Choi. Members witnessed actively for these gatherings, and the average attendance of 150-200 San Franciscans was a stark contrast to the empty Lions Club Hall which had greeted Miss Kim's group. Ron Pepper wrote:

> We have pictures in our scrapbook of the public meetings which the Japanese family has held. Since the San Francisco family was very small when I came these pictures really impressed me. . . . Of course I thought we could do the same thing here someday, but really doing it even with the comparatively small membership we have is something to give me great hope for our collective ability in the future.[37]

The student movement, training sessions, and public meetings all helped root the Re-Education Center. In short, the transplant was taking. There were, however, two other developments of 1968-69 which, while not without precedent in the Japanese church, led to a growth not previously seen.

International Exchange Press

One of the most important factors influencing the future direction of Mr. Choi's group was the establishment of the International Exchange Press in January, 1968. Unlike the American church's first print shop in Galen Pumphrey's bedroom, this new print company focused on outside jobs. It was the family's first business. A community newsletter explained Mr. Choi's idea:

> He said that it was time to begin to build the economic foundation for the ideal city where our brothers and sisters could live and work together. . . . "If we can work together in our own business, we can really feel that every effort is serving God 100% and what's more

> we can overcome the situation that exists when brothers
> and sisters hold outside jobs where people and
> environment make it difficult to practice and become
> truth. Also, we need to set up a business with the
> potential to really support the family economically."[38]

If the rationale was clear, it was not, at first, totally clear
what business enterprise was appropriate. As one member noted,
"There was much discussion and 'looking into' of the kind of
businesses that would serve our purposes best."[39] Then, in late
January, 1968, the "heavenly chance" came to purchase what
had been a one-man print shop in the poorer section of 3rd Street
in downtown San Francisco. Ron Pepper wrote, "We determined
to spend our sweat and tears to restore this world and gathered
$2000 within twelve hours to make the down payment."[40]

Although the shop was small, hopes were large. The printing
company would be only a first step, and as its name,
International Exchange Press implied, the vision was global.[41]
Regardless of the vision, opening a print shop necessitated many
practical tasks. One member wrote, "From that time on, the key
words and main focus of our family were: 'Witness! and bring
the printing orders!'"[42]

Mr. Choi, especially, began to focus more energy on the
company, and within a year the shop began to expand. Most of
the financial returns were reinvested to allow volume capacity to
increase, and orders that previously took many days to put out
could be done in a day. The shop went from two presses to five
and added other equipment. Most importantly, it was able to line
up regular customers.

In addition to outside jobs, the shop printed church literature.
As well as witnessing materials, the first *Universal Voice* was
printed in May, 1968. Conceived of as the community's
newspaper and published monthly, the *Universal Voice* became
increasingly sophisticated. On the other hand, the *Epoch-Maker*,
first published in April, 1969, was fashioned along the lines of
Miss Kim's *New Age Frontiers*. An internal newsletter, it
contained sermons, letters, news briefs and inspirational

material. While these published periodicals were significant, of more import as a formative influence were the booklets that Mr. Choi published. These launched the community into a radical new direction.

The Principles of Education

Aside from the decision to initiate business enterprises, the other major formative influence on the new community was the publication of Mr. Choi's *Principles of Education*. Unlike Miss Kim's text which was purported to be a pure translation of the Principles as lectured in Korea, Mr. Choi's work was a conscious adaptation. As such, it had significant impact on the direction in which the community was to move: specifically, from a theological to an educational and finally utopian focus. It is important to recognize that the Principle was the matrix of the community and was consistently taught. Nonetheless, to understand the distinctive development of the Re-Education Center, it is necessary to outline the origins, content, and implications of Mr. Choi's *Principles of Education*.

The *Principles of Education* were written by Mr. Choi to appeal to secular, non-theistic audiences. First composed in Japan where the Christian base was slight and where the Korean origins of the Principle had to be camouflaged, the series was revised and expanded in San Francisco. Thus, the same cultural context which led the community to organize as an educational foundation also fostered a revised ideology. As for the sources of this revision, Mr. Choi's words must suffice:

> I used the Divine Principle, which is a very religious approach. But I digested the Divine Principle. Based on the Divine Principle, I put my philosophical ideas and a little bit of oriental religion together and I a little bit changed the Divine Principle.[43]

A series of booklets published by the community during 1969, the *Principles of Education* elaborated specific theories of Mr. Choi: *Theory of Cause and Effect, Theory of Universal Value, Theory of Good and Evil, Theory of the Ideal Man, Theory of Happiness, The Purpose of Mankind.* Two titles contemplated but never written (or translated from the Japanese) were *Theory of the Kaleidoscopic Community* and *Theory of Eternity.* Basically, the series was a humanistic counterpart to the *Divine Principle.* Ancient wisdom was stressed over new revelation; the "human way of life" was stressed over transcendent grace; and human ignorance was emphasized over sin. In short, Mr. Choi's *Principles of Education* posited the attainability of an ideal world through an application of the community's overriding concept of conscientious common sense.

Although Mr. Choi devised a system of educational principles that would presumably lead to "divine" principles, what was critical for the community's development was the way in which the *Principles of Education* assumed a life of their own. Rather than leading to theology, the *Principles of Education* were set off against theology. Thus, the break between the new community in the Bay Area and the one that had preceded it was complete. As Mr. Choi later remarked, "My way is more a character-educational way, and Miss Kim's is more of a church-theological way."

Not only was there a break between the communities but there was a reaction against the previous interpretation of the Principle. In this sense, Mr. Choi's *Principles of Education* were constructed not only as a response to a particular secular environment but also as a response to the Principle. If Miss Kim responded to metaphysical truths reminiscent of Swedenborg and a personal healing, Mr. Choi responded to ethical truths and the possibility of social reconstruction. His emphasis on building institutions was particularly strong. Concluding his *Theory of the Ideal Man,* he wrote:

> Without concrete action, concrete ideals will never be
> realized and are useless. We are not only metaphysical
> existences, but we are also actual existences. Therefore,
> happiness comes from actualization of idea. Greater
> happiness comes from a greater actualization and
> attainment of ideals. So, understanding truth is
> something, but actualizing truth is everything.[44]

More than any other factor, the *Principles of Education* led
the community into a utopian experiment. Ironically, although
afraid of behaving like his father, Mr. Choi began building a
shrine of his own.

Founding the International Ideal City

By the end of 1969, the Re-Education Center was quite
successful and members could point to substantial growth. Mr.
Choi's *Principles of Education* were printed the previous October
and, as one piece of church literature noted, over 500,000
educational pamphlets had been distributed. The International
Exchange Press was turning over $24,000 worth of business a
month and included sophisticated equipment as well as ten
regular employees. As many as 270 San Franciscans had
attended the monthly Public Meetings and the *Universal Voice*
was circulating to 3,000 Bay Area residents. The Student
Movement continued to grow and was operating on state
campuses at Davis, Sacramento, Hayward, Santa Clara, and
Santa Cruz. A corps of lecturers were available and the
movement was also beginning to penetrate into high school
classrooms. A soon to be established "adult" center would
accommodate older associates. Perhaps the most accurate
measure of the center's growth was the annual financial
statement of the International Unification Church. From a total
income of $10,639 in May, 1968, the corporation was operating
on a budget of over a quarter of a million dollars by May,
1970.[45]

As a result of this rather phenomenal three and a half years of growth, group members found themselves at a turning point as the new decade of the 1970s began. The sense that they were ready for a new step was best depicted in Mr. Choi's move from San Francisco to Calistoga, California, about fifty miles northeast of the Bay Area, where the community had an A-frame house and twenty acres of land. There, amid the mineral baths and hot springs of the Napa Valley, Mr. Choi lived from January to March, 1970. Although this move had been prompted by a recurrence of health problems, it was in this somewhat isolated and idyllic setting that Mr. Choi formulated the next stage of the community's development. At a Family Meeting on March 12, 1970, he announced:

> From now on, we will increase our project to actualize the international ideal city based on our land in Calistoga. This is really good land but we will look for even more and better land . . . The centers are going to compete with each other from now on. We will send good men to our place in Calistoga. Later, we will expand, make our own city, our own bank and currency, our own everything. We will experiment. If we can establish the ideal city-system, we can win the whole world. [46]

Once this declaration was made, the community quickly found "more and better land." Alongside the masthead of the next *Epoch-Maker* ran the following:

> Bulletin: Our Family has just purchased 600 acres of land in Northern California, a couple of hours drive from San Francisco. Hills, streams, and beautiful farming lands are the foundations for our family's newest project: THE INTERNATIONAL IDEAL CITY.[47]

Located off Route 128 just south of Boonville in Mendocino County, California, the former Hiram Nobles Sheep Ranch was now the property of the Re-Education Center. While members were inspired by Edenic possibilities and tended to quote freely from the Book of Revelation, the same balance between spiritual and organizational authority that characterized the Re-Education Center also characterized the center's approach to the International Ideal City. On the one hand, members were 'pioneers' exploring the new land with a spirit of high adventure. On the other hand, they were 'scientists' organizing a utopian experiment that would 'prove' their social theories. To understand the story of the International Ideal City, it is necessary to balance their pioneer spirit with the test results.

The vision of founding an ideal city, a vision which Mr Choi articulated concretely while in Calistoga, was, in fact, the vision he had carried to the Bay Area from Japan. It had kept the community going during the early days in San Francisco, inspired the group's entry in business enterprises, and was now leading the community into a high-risk utopian venture. Although the group was able to raise the down-payment for the land through the donation of one member, they were heavily mortgaged. On the other hand, the community felt prepared to make the leap. As Mr Choi put it, "We must put forth great effort with a spirit of adventure."[48]

The spirit of adventure that Mr Choi had cultivated in his missionary life since first stowing away to Japan was re-activated in the Ideal City project. The community was going where they hadn't gone before. Whereas the Re-Education Center was based on the successful Japanese pattern, there was no pattern for an international ideal city. For this reason, no less than in Miss Kim's group, expectations were extravagant. Initial plans called for the city to "be composed of various sectors representing the unique architectural style of a particular culture: United States, Canada, Africa, the Nations of South America, Europe, the Middle East and Far East." Development of the project was to proceed in three discrete phases:

FIRST PHASE 1970 to 1971— Completion of agricultural project and educational/cultural buildings for training character and for workers living quarters. Necessary improvements on lower land to provide adequate roadways, bridge, etc.

SECOND PHASE 1971 to 1972— Implementation of international sector to include houses of each culture and international pioneer university together with research and computer facilities.

THIRD PHASE 1972 to 1973— Begin roadside shops for vegetables, hotel and restaurant facilities, expanded educational facilities, living quarters, and dam for recreational area.[49]

If the city had a timetable for completion of its physical plant, it also had a constitution that expressed its orientation and ideals. The basic ideals were expressed in the "Articles of Establishment of the International Ideal City" and included relevant sections on politics, economy, education, culture, law and "qualifications for citizenship."[50]

While it was a pioneer venture, the International Ideal City Project also was an experiment. As such, it was avowedly public. Just as Mr. Choi had refused a copyright for his *Principles of Education*, in order "to freely contribute to mankind" beyond group benefit, so too, the Ideal City Project would be a model for others to study. As one early report stated,

When the working model is established, psychologists, social scientists, teachers, industrial anthropologists, personnel directors, and politicians can visit the city and see how an ideal society works.[51]

What, then, would such researchers have had a chance to see? In March, 1970, they would have seen "600 acres of rolling hills and bottomland and two perennial streams, virgin except for a few acres of apple orchard." Two months later, in May, 1970, they would have seen "two house trailers with a sewage system, a dam, and a network of trenches irrigating ten acres planted with tomatoes, squash, corn, cucumbers, and pumpkins. In September, they would have seen "an elegant double-width mobile home" as well as pipes and sprinklers watering fields that had "just delivered the peak of their crops to Safeway."[52] A freshly dug well provided water for hot and cold taps, and a newly constructed chicken coop housed 1500 chickens. Two hundred sheep roamed the hills while five cattle roamed the bottomland.

These results were impressive for the first six months of ownership. However, this was the extent of the physical development of the Ideal City. Had researchers come back six months later, they would have seen much the same thing. Although county authorities had approved plans for a first educational building, that structure was never built. Nor, though Mr. Choi had planted fifty grape leaves before the entrance to the planned hotel, was that hotel or any other building ever constructed.

Undoubtedly, had researchers been present, they would have questioned why progress was halted. Overall, there were two major factors. The first had to do with the nature of experimental enterprises. Although the community had invested heavily in the project, it was never a pioneer struggle or a matter of survival but rather an experiment in social theory. The objective distance maintained throughout was evident in the fact that at no time did the community commit more than eight to fifteen of its one hundred members to full-time work on the site.

The second factor followed from a new gestalt which the project had created. The spirit of adventure refused to be confined to Mendocino County and permeated community activities in the Bay Area. As members quickly discovered, "Everyone really opens when there is talk of our land and the city."[53] In this sense, the experiment began to transform the experimenters and to reshape community life. Witnessing became largely a matter of promoting the land development with brochures, mailings and tables set up in the city. The Public Meetings, which had been switched from the Unitarian Center to the Scottish Rite Temple, became fund-raisers for the project.

If the experiment re-shaped community activities in the city, it too was transformed. A kind of dialectical process evolved whereby the project was not only an experiment but a great site for weekend training sessions and festivals. With land, the community found that it didn't have to rent sites for public gatherings but could host their own. The center initiated "Open Land" programs inviting Boonville residents and San Franciscans to the project for a day of "activities, entertainment, open-air meals, and conversation."[54] Instead of a new educational building, a new outdoor stage was constructed by International Ideal City Ranch carpenter, Bobby Wilson.

In short, rather than a discrete experiment, members integrated the International Ideal City with activities of the Re-Education Center. To assess the success or failure of the experiment, it is necessary to consider the transformation of the Re-Education Center.

The International Re-Education Foundation

As mentioned, the founding of the International Ideal City had important ramifications for the community in San Francisco. It not only affected how the community went about its activities but also affected how the group thought about itself. It altered the community's self-image. This was most apparent in the transformation of the "Re-Education Center" into the "International Re-Education Foundation." The group no longer thought of itself as a local center but as an international foundation. The new foundation was incorporated by the state of California on May 4, 1971.

Thus, the founding of the International Ideal City in Mendocino County was answered by the founding of the

International Re-Education Foundation (IRF) in San Francisco. In many ways, the new foundation mirrored the natural growth of the Re-Education Center. International Exchange Enterprises had proliferated beyond one printing company to an employment agency, a travel service, a home-restoration company, an import-export venture, a gas station, and a cleaning company.[55] Within the community, "house organization" had proliferated into twelve discrete departments with individual heads. The *Universal Voice* had expanded its format, and the New Age Band had evolved into the New Age Orchestra.

At the same time, the International Re-Education Foundation was more than the Re-Education Center writ large. There were qualitative as well as quantitative changes. Basically, these qualitative changes meant *less* family and *more* organization. Although Papasan and Mamasan were still present, organizational demands of the expanded foundation created a more formal and public atmosphere. Previously informal question and answer sessions with Mr. Choi were now titled "Wisdom from the East" and open to the public. There was less time for family activity as every night of the week was tied up. Mondays were set aside for "Unification Principle lectures & discussion"; Tuesdays were "Wisdom from the East" nights; Wednesdays were "Fellowship" nights; Thursdays were "World Culture" nights; Fridays were "Comparative Religion" nights; Saturdays were "Current Affairs" nights and Sundays were meeting days.[56]

Equally illustrative of the move from family to organization were the opportunities for new members to contribute to the activities of the International Re-Education Foundation. They could, as one piece of literature put it,

> ____   play in the New Age Orchestra
> ____   sing in the New Age Choir
> ____   participate in the New Age Players (help with props, costumes, scenery, etc. as well as acting)
> ____   collect money for dinner or special events

    ____   be a doorman one night a week

    ____   help in the kitchen (main dishes, desserts & breads)

    ____   be a waitress in the coffee shop

    ____   type

    ____   help with art projects (drawing, lettering posters, flyers, etc.)

    ____   be an After-Dinner volunteer

    ____   drive people home after the evening's program

    ____   help mail out the Universal Voice

    ____   provide entertainment for Open House, World Family Meetings, banquets, etc.

    ____   help organize banquets, cultural events & other special events

    ____   be active in making new friends of the Foundation

    ____   bake for the coffee shop, birthdays or festivals.

The move from family to organization was concretized by the purchase of an imposing new headquarters at 44 Page Street, San Francisco in June, 1971. The former site of a Druid Temple, the new Page Street building was four stories high with a ballroom and balcony as well as office space and numerous rooms. It was to the community in the urban environment what the land project was to the community in rural Mendocino County. It provided a facility for extensive programs. At the same time, the building was reminiscent of Miss Kim's group's purchase of the Masonic Avenue house and required extensive renovation. Nonetheless, the Page Street headquarters quickly became a center of activity.

One of the important effects of the Page Street purchase was its impact on associate membership. The potential of the new facility to enhance outside involvement was considerable. The large kitchen was made available for luncheons in the afternoon. Meeting rooms were available for rent in the evenings. One could become an associate member for $2.00 a month and be entitled "to all publications, attendance and dinner at the monthly

birthday celebration, and a visitor's pass to the International
Ideal City."[57] For $35.00, associate members could have dinner
every night of the month at the main center. For a larger
donation, associates could become a foundation sponsor.
Although the Buchannan Street Adult center was sold to help
purchase Page Street headquarters, the "World Family
Movement" was organized to involve adults and parents of
members. The foundation was consciously attempting to increase
its contacts within the local community.

The Page Street facility also led the community to two more
ambitious projects. These transformed what had been the Student
Movement and the Public Meeting. What resulted consummated
the efforts of Mr. Choi's group in the San Francisco Bay Area.

The International Pioneer Academy

If the establishment of the International Ideal City was on
Mr. Choi's agenda from the beginning of his stay in the Bay
Area, closely linked to that vision was the setting up of a
university. Although it was not financially feasible to begin
construction of a university on the land in Mendocino County,
purchase of the Page Street facility gave a new impetus to the
idea. By setting up "The International Pioneer Academy" at 44
Page Street, Mr. Choi not only actualized that idea but also
transformed the Student Movement. Rather than operating in
nearby universities, students would attend their own! Again, as
with the ideal city, the move was toward a reformation of society
through the establishment of model institutions that worked. In
the context of campus riots and disillusionment of the late 1960s
and early 1970s, the Re-Education Foundation nurtured hopes of
remaking society through character education of future leaders.
This attitude was reflected in the "Prospectus for the
Establishment" of the International Pioneer Academy:

> Political experts alone will not bring about a better
> society and world. The realization of such a society will

> be accomplished by capable leaders who are guided by principle and who have character and human dignity. Without an education to create such leaders, the idea of a better society and world is just a dream, and the suffering of humanity cannot be solved. Such an educational academy of leaders can be the rock on which to build a great new society.[58]

An advisory meeting was held at 44 Page Street on June 7, 1971 with "much discussion" about the forthcoming International Pioneer University. The *Universal Voice* announced that the academy would open for its first semester in the fall.

Having made that commitment, the next step was to recruit faculty. Although a formidable task, the assignment was somewhat mollified by the already existent Student Movement. Not only were members active on Bay Area campuses but also their experimental courses had been well received. In addition, the Student Center had, since January 1970, instituted a Friday night "Forum of Giants" which brought professors to the center. Combined with the steady stream of speakers for the foundation's scheduled programs, a pool of contacts was available.

In addition, the idea of founding an academy was itself enticing. Dedicated as "a battleground against partial ideas and a catalyst for their synthesis," the Academy was as attractive to emeritus professors with careers behind them as it was to "up-and-comers" with hypotheses to test. By September, the foundation had recruited an impressive array of scholars. Headed by R. Gordon Agnew, Professor Emeritus at the University of California Medical Center, who accepted the post of president, the faculty included Dr. Haridas Chaudhuri, founder of the California Institute of Asian Studies, as well as eight Bay Area professors, a lawyer and the news producer for KRON-TV.[59]

More problematic than the recruitment of faculty was the recruitment of students. Although scholarships were available for the $300.00 per term tuition, the academy was not chartered and could not offer degrees. Significantly, by late summer, as one member's diary noted, "most potential students had already picked a college or university to attend for the upcoming academic year."[60] Nonetheless, by mid-September, the foundation recruited ten outside students who, along with twenty or so members, comprised the Academy's first class.

The International Pioneer Academy officially opened on September 20, 1971. Course offerings were available in the History of World Cultures, Fine Arts, Sociology, Economics, Law, History of World Philosophy, History of World Religions, Psychology, Political Science, Nations of the World, Contemporary Ideological Currents, Contemporary International and Domestic Problem Analysis, and the *Principles of Education*. Classes met from 8:00 a.m. until 11:50 a.m. (with breaks) Monday through Friday, from 7:30 p.m. until 9:20 p.m. Monday through Wednesday, and from 7:30 p.m. until 8:20 p.m. on Thursday when Mr. Choi lectured. Besides the uniforms which students wore, each day began with several songs and a pledge of allegiance to the U.S. flag. On the entrance of each professor, the class, as one member wrote, "would all rise and say, 'Good morning, Mr./Dr. (teacher's name),' to show respect."[61]

Overall, Mr. Choi achieved a rather remarkable coup in establishing the International Pioneer Academy. Not only was he able to integrate "universal guiding principles" into the academy's curriculum and framework, but also he was able to involve important outside people in its development. At the same time, he was able to integrate the academy with the International Ideal City Project. There, students would be able to put into practice theories learned in the classroom. It was, of course, the addition of 44 Page Street that enabled Mr. Choi to parley the Student Movement into the International Pioneer Academy. The same facility effected a similar transformation of the Public Meeting.

International Friendship Banquets

As previously mentioned, public meetings sponsored by the Re-Education Center at the San Francisco Unitarian Center were, with the purchase of the Boonville property, transformed into "fundraisers" at the Scottish Rite Auditorium and finally into "Open Land" programs hosted by the community in Mendocino County. They continued following the establishment of the International Re-Education Foundation and became linked with seasonal celebrations. "International" spring, summer, and fall festivals were held in 1971. These festivals were elaborate affairs featuring participation from "Booners" (residents of Boonville or surrounding towns and counties), San Franciscans and international representatives from various of the consulates in San Francisco.[62] With such sponsors as Sheriff Matthew Carberry of San Francisco, Mrs. Margaret Krsak Koesen and Homer Mannix, editor and publisher of the *Anderson Valley Advertiser*, the gatherings included country concessions, art exhibitions, pony rides, speeches, athletic contests, international song and dance, and tours of the Ideal City Project.

If the land in Mendocino demonstrated to the community the possibilities of hosting their own rural gatherings, the purchase of 44 Page Street offered similar possibilities in the city. With ballroom and balcony, the new facility became the site of a succession of "International Friendship Banquets" during the latter half of 1971. The first of these, "German-American Friendship Night" was held on June 12, 1971. It featured a program of dinner, entertainment, cultural discussions and dancing as well as speeches by Dr. Erich Franz Sommer, First Class Consul, Cultural Affairs, for the German Consulate, and San Francisco Sheriff Matthew Carberry.

"Italian-American Friendship Night" on July 10 was an even more elaborate affairs with 500 guests, a flag ceremony, speeches by San Francisco Mayor Joseph Alioto and the Honorable Piero Mustacchi, Vice Consul of Italy. It also included a dance presentation from the San Francisco Park and

Recreation Department and music by representatives from the San Francisco Conservatory of Music as well as the Foundation's own New Age Band and String Quartet. Mayor Alioto returned to 44 Page Street on August 28, 1971, for "Japanese -American Friendship Night" and was again a featured speaker along with Japanese Consul General Eikichi Hara. The foundation sponsored "India-American Friendship Night" on October 23rd. Tickets for all these programs were sold at $3.50 each by members who witnessed actively to make sure each event was a sellout.[63]

Besides bi-national friendship banquets, the Foundation sponsored other public gatherings at 44 Page Street. Noteworthy was the "World Religion Congregation" held on August 8, 1971. Opening with a "universal proclamation of peace," the program had speakers from seven major faiths: Ali Kahn—Islam; Rabbi Paul Citrin—Judaism; Dr. Framroze Bode—Zoroastrianism; Rev. Koshin Ogui—Buddhism; Rev. Tony Ubalde—Christianity; Dr. Haridas Chaudhuri—Buddhism; and Sang Ik Choi—Universalism.[64] As with all programs, the World Religion Congregation concluded with foundation members joined together on the stage in song. On August 21, 1971, the Foundation sponsored "Family Night" for parents, children, aunts, uncles, and cousins of members, and on November 6th, they sponsored "Utopia Night." Combined with what had gone before, the last Page Street banquet of 1971 was aptly titled.

Final Success

If the autumn of 1963 marked a harvest of sorts for Miss Kim's group in the Bay Area, the latter half of 1971 was harvest-time for Mr. Choi's group. Besides founding the International Pioneer Academy and successfully implementing International Friendship Banquets, numerous businesses, and an expanded nightly program, Mr. Choi and the foundation began to receive public recognition. Mr. Choi was named "Man of the Day" by a local radio station. More significantly, on June 7,

1971, members learned that the Federal Government's Alternative Service Program approved the foundation as "an acceptable alternate service to the draft for conscientious objectors."[65] In addition to public recognition, the foundation felt itself sufficiently evolved by the latter half of 1971 to sponsor a week-long "International Friendship Aloha Tour" to Hawaii beginning on August 23rd, a Human Relationship Symposium on October 30-31, and a full operatic production of *Madame Butterfly* on December 5th.[66]

While each of these occasions were noteworthy, they were all overshadowed by the "International Christmas Friendship Banquet" held December 18 1971 at the Kabuki Theater, 1881 Post Street in San Francisco. Again, if Children's Day 1963 was the culmination of Miss Kim's efforts in the Bay Area, the International Christmas Friendship Banquet of 1971 was the culmination of Mr. Choi's work. The previous year, well over six hundred San Franciscans, including seventy who had to be turned away, attended a similar foundation-sponsored Christmas banquet at Bimbo's Restaurant near Fisherman's Wharf in San Francisco. The Kabuki Theater, however, was able to accommodate the over twelve hundred guests who paid $6.50 each to attend the 1971 International Christmas Friendship Banquet.

Co-chaired by Lim P. Lee, postmaster of San Francisco, Glenn Bassett, vice president of Wells Fargo Bank, and Dr. Robert Thornton, professor of physics at the University of San Francisco, the second annual International Christmas Friendship Festival was intended to be "a proclamation of peace, goodwill, and love among world peoples." Thirty-seven nations were officially represented in an opening flag ceremony and by their consular representatives. Performances by entertainers from eight nations as well as an evening overture by the New Age Orchestra of the International Re-Education Center highlighted the program. In addition to international representation, state and civic officials were on hand for the occasion. Senator Milton Marks extended a welcome, and addressing the audience on "The

Possibility of World Peace" were Mrs. Homai Framroze Bode, recipient of the "Member of the British Empire" award for distinguished social work; Dr. Zuretti L. Goosby, president of San Francisco's Board of Education; and George Mardikian, recipient of the Medal of Freedom, author of the noted "Song of America" and founder of the city's internationally known Omar Khayyam's Restaurant.[67]

The International Christmas Friendship Banquet was truly climactic for members of the Re-Education Foundation in the sense that all aspects of their work came together at the Kabuki Theater. On March 12, 1970, when Mr. Choi held the family meeting that launched the community into the International Ideal City Project, he commented that the group had "a basic weak point, a lack of good connections or contacts."[68] As members gathered on the stage of the Kabuki Theater and looked out over the audience of prominent San Franciscans and world delegates, that weak point appeared to be overcome.

Despite that prospect, the Re-Education Foundation was not to enter the promised land of utopian fulfillment. As was the case with Miss Kim's group, the culmination of their activity was also a turning point. The next three years would bring dramatic changes to the Unification Church in the San Francisco Bay Area. The most obvious of these changes was the dismantling of all Mr. Choi had built up.

NOTES

1. *Prospectus for the Establishment of the International Ideal City Under the Re-Education Movement.* Pamphlet published by the Re-Education Center, 1970.

2. Michiko Matsumoto, "The Road Rev. Nishikawa Followed," *Faith and Life* (Tokyo: Kougensha, 1976). Unpublished English translation.

3. Tenrikyo ("The Religion of Heavenly Truth") was founded by Nakayama Miki (1798-1887) following a revelatory experience in 1838. It was granted government sanction in 1908 as the last of the original thirteen Shinto sects. In 1960, Tenrikyo withdrew from the order of Association of Shinto Sects as a consequence of its intended universal mission. Followers believe salvation extends over the world from a sacred spot called the Jiba—the center of the world—situated in the city of Tenri, Nara prefecture. There, followers have constructed Tenri-city, the model of the ideal society which they were commissioned to build on earth. See Joseph M. Kitagawa, *Religion in Japanese History* (New York: Columbia University Press, 1966), pp. 220-272, 308-310; H. Weill McFarland, *The Rush Hour of the Gods* (New York: The Macmillan Company, 1967), pp. xi-xii, 58-59, 89; Robert S. Ellwood, "Tenrikyo, The Religion of Heavenly Wisdom," *The Eagle and the Rising Sun: Americans and the New Religions of Japan* (Philadelphia: The Westminster Press, 1974), pp. 37-68; Hori Ichiro (ed.), *Japanese Religion* (Tokyo: Kodansha International Ltd., 1972).

4. Matsumoto, "The Road Rev. Nishikawa Followed."

5. Ibid.

6. Ibid.

7. Ibid.

8. Masaru Nishikawa [Sang Ik Choi], "The Record of Witnessing in Japan," in *Faith and Life* (Tokyo: Kougensha, 1966). Unpublished English translation.

9. Matsumoto, "The Road Rev. Nishikawa Followed."

10. Nishikawa, "The Record of Witnessing in Japan."

11. Matsumoto, "The Road Rev. Nishikawa Followed."

12. Nishikawa, "The Record of Witnessing in Japan."

13. "News from Japan," *New Age Frontiers*, April 1963.

14. Interview with Sang Ik Choi at Alamo, California, October, 1978.

15. "Report from Japan: Economic Enterprises," *New Age Frontiers*, February 1966.

16. "Report from Japan: Organization," *New Age Frontiers*, February 1966.

17. "Report from Japan: Training Programs," *New Age Frontiers*, February, 1966.

18. Student riots erupted throughout Korea.

19. "Report from Japan: University Division," *New Age Frontiers*, February, 1966.

20. Ibid.

21. Matsumoto, "The Road Rev. Nishikawa Followed."

22. David Doerring, "History of the Re-Education Center," *Epoch Maker*, March, 1969.

23. Interview with Koro Ishiguro, Alamo, California, March 1979.

24. Doerring, "History of the Re-Education Center," Epoch Maker, March 1969.

25. Ibid.

26. Ibid.

27. "Spiritual Revival," *Universal Voice* , May 1968.

28. Interview with Sang Ik Choi, Alamo, California, March 1979.

29. Edna Lee, "The Family," unpublished paper, San Francisco State University, n.d.

30. Interview with Sang Ik Choi, Alamo, California, March 1979.

31. Alice Hamaker, "What's Happening," *Epoch Maker* #15, October 1979.

32. "Prospectus for the Establishment of the Student Unification Movement," *Universal Voice*, October 1968.

33. Ron Pepper, untitled testimony, *Universal Voice*, July 1968.

34. Carmela Acohido, "Third Successful Session," *Universal Voice*, September 1968.

35. Ron Pepper, "Training Session," *Epoch Maker* #9, July 1969.

36. "Re-Education Center 6th Training Session," unpublished manual, n.d.

37. Ron Pepper, "The Past Year: 1969," *Epoch Maker* #18, January 1970.

38. "International Exchange Press," *Universal Voice*, August 1968.

39. Ibid .

40. Ron Pepper, "History of the Re-Education Center," *Epoch Maker* #2, April 1969.

41. According to the *Universal Voice*, August 1968, "The opening of the International Exchange Press (then called the World Printing Company) was unheralded by the mass media, but in the hearts and minds of brothers and sisters that day, had great historical significance and meaning. Only they recognized how much the growth and development—the success—of that small 'seed of a company' would mean to this world someday. This was the first printing company established in America whose sole purpose for existence was not in any way for the selfish gain of its workers or management. It was established for the benefit of America and the American people."

42. Josephine Louie, "History of the Re-Education Center," *Epoch Maker* #4, April 1969.

43. Interview with Sang Ik Choi, Alamo, California, March 1969.

44. Sang Ik Choi, *The Theory of the Ideal Man* (San Francisco: Re-Education Center, 1969), 49.

45. *Prospectus for the Establishment of the International Ideal City*, brochure published in 1971.

46. Sang Ik Choi, "Papasan Speaks at Family Meeting March 12, 1970," *Epoch Maker* #21, March 1970.

47. Bulletin," *Epoch Maker* #21, March 1970.

48. Sang Ik Choi, "Papasan Speaks at Family Meeting March 12, 1970."; The center had committed itself to a $165,000 mortgage on the property. They had been able to pay the downpayment through a donation from Ellie Elliot, a member from San Jose.

49. *Prospectus for the Establishment of the International Ideal City*.

50. Ibid .

51. William McClellan, "Utopian Born: Extrovert Community Shows Practical Ways to Better World," *Universal Voice*, June 1970.

52. William McClellan, "New World Discovered," *Columbus: The Magazine for the 1970 San Francisco Columbus Day Celebration*, October, 1970

53. Michael Warder, "Letter from Mission in Palo Alto," *Epoch Maker #21*, March 1970.

54. Walter Gottesman, "Open Land Opens People," *Universal Voice*, September 1970.

55. These were International Exchange Employment, Seno Travel Service, Ideal Home Restoration, International Exchanges, International Exchange Union 76 Service Station, and International Exchange Maintenance.

56. *Prospectus for the Establishment of the International Re-Education Foundation*," brochure published in 1971.

57. "What Is the International Re-Education Foundation?" Brochure published in 1971.

58. "*Prospectus for the Establishment of the International Pioneer Academy*," brochure published in 1971.

59. "International Pioneer Academy: Global Education," *Universal Voice*, October 1971.

60. Kevin Brennan, "When and After Kevin Brennan First Met the Unified Family." Unpublished diary, 1967-70.

61. Ibid.

62. "International Summer Festival Held in Mendocino," *Universal Voice*, August 1971.

63. See "Cultures Come Together," *Universal Voice*, July 1971; and "Alioto Addresses Cultural Gathering," *Universal Voice*, August 1971.

64. "Major Religions Unite for World Cooperation," *Universal Voice* August 1971.

65. Selective Service System, California Headquarters. Letter to International Re-Education Foundation, June 7, 1971.

66. See "Schedule of Coming Events," *Epoch Maker #32-41*, July-November, 1971.

67. "Peace on Earth," *Universal Voice*, January 1972.

68. "Papasan Speaks at Family Meeting, March 12, 1970," *Epoch Maker*, #21, March 1970.

CHAPTER FIVE

A NATIONAL MOVEMENT ATTEMPTS TO EMERGE: 1966–71

A National Movement Attempts to Emerge—The Berkeley Center—Rev. Moon's Second World Tour—Reconsolidation—United Faith, Inc.

Although Mr. Choi's Re-Education Foundation was the dominant presence of the Unification Church in the San Francisco Bay Area during the late 1960s and beginning years of the 1970s, his Re-Education Foundation (later the International Re-Education Foundation) was only one of three regional developments of the Unification Church in America. Miss Kim, after leaving the Bay Area in late 1965, directed the "Unified Family" of Washington, D.C., as well as a fluctuating network of centers throughout the United States. David Kim, while a Job Corps supervisor at Clearfield, Utah, continued to direct the Northwest family under the aegis of United Faith, Inc. More commonly referred to as Miss Kim's, Mr. Choi's and Mr. Kim's groups, the Unification Church in America during this period consisted of three independent corporations, each with its own newsletter, interpretation of the Principle, and membership.

The Bay Area continued to be significant as by the end of 1971, all three groups were represented there. The International Re-Education Foundation was at the zenith of its development in

San Francisco. The Berkeley center, Miss Kim's Bay Area
remnant, had grown rapidly and by 1971 was having a
significant impact. Finally, Oakland chapel activities were
intensified with the return of David Kim to the Bay Area in
February, 1971. A tale of three cities emerged with the Bay
Area as a possible focal point for the resolution of regional
divisions and a source of national thrust.

However, rather than a focal point of unity, the Bay Area
became a focal point of confrontation among the three groups.
Disparate methods of proselytization, interpretations of the
Principle, and overall style led to mutual suspicion, distrust and
lack of communication. Although focused locally, there was little
sense in which the Bay Area would serve as the locus for the
resolution of missionary conflicts. If anything, differences were
intensified in the close proximity of missionary groups to one
another.

As a prelude to rounding out a treatment of the Unification
Church prior to 1972, it is necessary to explore the interrelations
among the three missionary groups. The best way to do so is
through a consideration of the several attempts to forge a
national movement during this period. While these attempts were
not successful, they did highlight, often dramatically, the crucial
role of the San Francisco Bay Area for any unifying thrust. The
first such effort followed Rev. Moon's 1965 world tour.

A National Movement Attempts to Emerge

Having decided to re-locate in Washington, D.C., following
completion of her 1965 world tour with Rev. Moon, Miss Kim
arrived there in the midst of a two-week "Mid-Winter Training
Conference." Col. Bo Hi Pak opened the conference with the
assertion that they were "assembling God's army for training and
preparation in the battles to come." In a deeper sense, the
conference served to convene various diaspora centers scattered
across the states as a result of the earlier exodus out of the Bay

Area. Members arrived at "Fellowship House" in Washington, D.C., from New York City, Cleveland, Texas, Oklahoma, and Philadelphia. The real purpose of the gathering was to kick off national headquarters. One member wrote:

> At first our hearts were light and gay with all our brothers and sisters, and our security among ourselves. But as time wore on, we heard of the plans for the U.S. headquarters and the problems involved; our talk changed. As the lectures progressed and the questions rolled out, our belts tightened.[1]

The most serious problem which Miss Kim addressed in her "Message for 1966" was the style of center life which had evolved during her absence. Miss Kim admonished:

> I want to make a few remarks for those in the United States. Some members still seem to be interested in developing ESP; they fast and meditate a great deal. For the past long period of preparation for this new age, people had but to meditate and fast a certain amount. However, the new age has now dawned and we are in the Age of Action. . . .
>
> We must use our common sense on these points. We must cultivate our common sense in the light of the Divine Principle. Then the common sense will become a better and more wholesome guide than ESP. I want you to equip yourselves with deep and broad understanding of the truth, rather than depending on ESP.[2]

Noting in her message that Rev. Moon had commanded the group in Korea to double their membership in a three month period following his return, Miss Kim called on the American church to "parallel the movement in Korea, praying and working for the same goal." In this spirit, the national movement was launched.

Headed by Jim Fleming, who succeeded Gordon Ross as President of HSA-UWC and who preceded Miss Kim from the Bay Area to Washington, D.C., members organized a national staff. Not surprisingly, the February, 1966, issue of *New Age Frontiers* carried a lengthy "Report from Japan," detailing among other items their highly evolved national structure and subsequent growth. The implications were obvious. By April, Miss Kim left on a "swing through eastern U.S." drumming up support for the national organization.

Despite these developments, the newly emergent national movement faced two formidable obstacles. The first and most obvious of these involved opposition from rival missionaries. The second, while less obvious, was finally more devastating, and stemmed from the problems Miss Kim referred to in her new year address.

Opposition from rival missionaries.

Predictably, the establishment of national headquarters in Washington, D.C., was viewed with suspicion by other missionary groups, especially David Kim's Northwest group. Whether in response to the East Coast "Mid-Winter Training Conference" or to the establishment of headquarters, the Northwest family inaugurated its own "Monthly Training Conference for the training of Northwest Leaders" in January, 1966. Gathering for three days every month in either Portland or Seattle, members from those cities as well as Eugene, Vancouver, B.C., and Boise devoted themselves to lectures, study and comprehensive examinations based on *Individual Preparation for His Coming Kingdom: Interpretation of the Principles*, by David S.C.Kim. This translation was normative in his group until 1972.

If there was any question as to Mr. Kim's group's attitude toward the newly-formed national headquarters, all uncertainty was gone by early spring, 1966. As Miss Kim toured centers in the eastern states, the *United Temple Bulletin*, official news organ of the Northwest group, featured a lengthy editorial entitled, "Expressed Opinions on so called 'National Headquarters', Washington, D.C., by the Northwest Families." Noting "pressure from this newly established headquarters toward local centers and also to the Northwest Chapel," the article listed a five-point critique:

1. Membership on a piece of paper means nothing until we can unite in heart and mind.
2. The departments and functions are vague and ambiguous, lacking in practical application to the situations in this country.
3. It is felt that the Board of Directors should be composed of a more equal number from each group. As it is presently set up, there is no guarantee that the group having the most members on the board will not use dictatorial methods in running the body. The members from the other groups will have little or no say on the board.
4. Most members strongly opposed the propositions set down by Wash., D.C., on tests, certificates, and membership. They feel they are already in the Heavenly family. How can one become a member by only sending in a subscription to the Washington body? Each missionary should exercise their own test system. The proposition set down on certificates, etc, are not acceptable.
5. It was agreed not to send letters of disagreement at this time to Washington, D.C. but rather to wait until Our Master comes and then certain points can be clarified.[3]

Besides these five summary points, the article included more vitriolic comments from individual members. One charged the new headquarters with "definite attempts very recently to split and destroy the Northwest Family, rather than to unite." Another asserted, "From the beginning the so called National Headquarters in Washington, D.C. has shown by their dictatorial methods that they will dictate to us our methods of teaching, preaching, etc., even to the extent of telling us we cannot use certain words." Against this backdrop, Mr. Kim's own comments were more conciliatory:

> From the beginning, when I started this work in 1959 in Oregon, we had different methods and opinions than those of the San Francisco group, most of whom are now in Washington, D.C. The ideas on the methods of doing this work are slightly different, but the goal is the same. . . .
> The Korean missionaries, including myself, should give up their old attitudes and reconceptualize the whole thing and meet together on an equal basis and with mutual understanding and true love in order to solve many years old problems.[4]

Although conciliatory, David Kim, nonetheless, stood firmly for coordination and cooperation among the groups rather than centralization.

Interestingly, the *United Temple Bulletin* article also included comments of Sang Ik Choi who had recently begun work in San Francisco. Mr. Choi also opted for local autonomy:

> Because of the different individual personalities and educational backgrounds of each missionary, their teaching methods are different. This fact plus the characteristic nature of the American continent makes it impossible to have formal unity in structure and administrative fields.[5]

Mr. Choi also responded to Jim Fleming's March 30, 1966, letter addressed to all American families, saying,

> The Korean missionaries cannot be under the American president or any chairman. They are equally assigned the right to say and right to preach without any disturbance from any other source.

> Jim's letter gives the impression that he will rule all
> things in the U.S. I have to say truth to the American
> family because there is lots of conflict on this matter of
> unity. I think, personally, there is no disunity, but as in
> any organization there are disagreements which are not
> necessarily bad, but in order to progress we need
> different opinions. We must not say [any] one is Satan
> because he does not agree.[6]

Internal problems

If opposition from rival missionaries stymied the newly
emergent national movement from its inception, internal
problems beleaguered headquarters as it attempted to evolve. It
would take more than organization to overcome the kinds of
difficulties referred to by Miss Kim in her New Year's message.
Rather than exciting testimonies from the field, by September,
1966, the *New Age Frontiers* was publishing such article reprints
as "Five Ways to Combat Depression" and calling on outlying
centers to make regular reports. By November, the problem was
recognized to originate less in outlying centers than in
headquarters itself. As one member put it,

> Because of the importance of Washington Center as
> National Headquarters, Satan has been very busy and
> has successfully held this Center in a virtual state of
> immobility. Many sobering discussions on this subject
> have marked recent months. The Executive Committee
> determined that Satan has taken enough, so the stage is
> being set for an all out attack. [7]

Ironically, this "all out attack" took the form of more
organization. Philip Burley was called to Washington, D.C. in
December, 1966, to head the Field Operations department. The
Field Operations Department was only one of five newly created
departments. Others were Administration, Publications, Public
Relations, and Business Enterprises. Combined with the election

of national officers for 1966-67, there was renewed hope. One New York member enthused,

> My brothers and sisters, it is true! The tide is turning, there is a new sense of mobilization. A sense of drawing up the forces for a new confrontation. There is a sense of transition from one state of activity to a higher, fuller one.[8]

Such hopes, however, were largely illusionary, and the discrepancy between organizational initiatives and concrete results produced casualties. The first casualty was Jim Fleming, whose March 1, 1967, resignation as president was accepted at a special session of the board of directors in Washington, D.C., on March 8th. Lowell Martin, from Oakland, California, and national vice-President, West, was unanimously elected by the board to complete Jim Fleming's term of office. Although hope was again generated, particularly in the area of economic expansion, by the end of 1967, Lowell Martin also was a casualty and was succeeded by Philip Burley. It was clear that national headquarters was faltering.

The Berkeley Center

If Miss Kim still asserted in a January, 1968, *New Age Frontiers* feature article that "Washington Center serves as U.S. Headquarters of our movement as well as nerve center of the entire Western World,"[9] it was equally clear that the movement had changed. For the remainder of the 1960s, Washington was not the hub of a national movement but a vigorous and successfully operating local center. Rather than extending its grasp across the country, the Washington Center became an example for other Unified Families to follow. It is in this context that the Washington Center influenced Bay Area developments through the Berkeley Center.

Of those centers subscribing to the Washington pattern, none were more successful than the Berkeley Center. At the same time, none were more closely connected to Washington. These ties were evident in the three founding members of the Berkeley Center: Edwin Ang, a Chinese doctoral student in economics at the University of California at Berkeley and 1962 convert of Miss Kim's original Bay Area group; Farley Jones, a Princeton University graduate, former law student and Washington Center member whom Miss Kim sent out to help in November, 1967; and Betsy O'Neill, a graduate student in psychiatric nursing at Columbia University whom Miss Kim sent out in June, 1968.

Originally housed in a single bedroom apartment, the Berkeley Center expanded to a three room flat and eight members by the end of 1968; to two houses and twenty-one members by the end of 1969; and to three centers housing forty members by the end of 1970. In June of 1970, Edwin Ang declared, "the call in Berkeley is for full scale advance along four major lines of attack; through spiritual activities, through business, through education, and through political involvement."[10] This fourfold division tells the story of the Berkeley Center's development as well as its connection to Washington.

Witnessing and Center Life

Prior to Farley Jones' arrival in Berkeley, Edwin Ang's main spiritual activity had been "survival." [11] Following Farley and Betsy's arrival, however, a new era of active evangelization began in the Berkeley Center. As Farley later noted, "we just put in hours of witnessing, hours of teaching, a lot of fasting and it was very exciting."[12] This evangelistic thrust was reflected in a letter of Jeff Tallakson, a former Campus Crusade for Christ affiliate and new member, who wrote,

> The most important of our goals for 1969 is witnessing, because this is the basis upon which our purpose here in Berkeley rests. We must advance upon Satan's front

line so we can be creative behind the lines. We are
developing new ways of witnessing and finding new
battlegrounds.[13]

These developments were consistent with the Washington
pattern. There, twelve dedicated new members moved into the
center by the end of 1968. The new emphasis was not on
national mobilization but on daily efforts and patience. Philip
Burley wrote,

> In our life there are high points of joy and success and
> creativity, but the major pattern is the day-today small,
> steady progress. Often this does not seem to show great
> results, and it is easy to get discouraged. But it is only
> through this steadfastness that we can remain
> faithful.[14]

At the same time, there were innovations. In Washington, a
"witno-bus" method had been adopted with members piling into
the center van for after-dinner and weekend forays on nearby
college campuses. Later, "witno-captains" led Washington
members on "witno-ventures" into laundromats, the National
Zoo, and airports.

The Washington pattern of center life was also influential on
the Berkeley Center. Having closed the gap on Washington in
terms of membership, the Berkeley Center also strove to draw
closer in terms of organization. As one member wrote in an
August, 1969, report "We began establishing a more basic
pattern of Family life, largely following Washington's
example."[15] By June, 1970, three days were regularly set aside
for specific purposes: Sundays for morning sermons, trips to
Holy Ground and practice teaching sessions for new teachers in
the evening; Wednesday evenings for a mid-week hour of
prayer, including reading and song; and Saturdays for morning
cleaning, afternoon witnessing and evening Principle Study
sessions from xerox copies of Mr. Eu's newly translated, though
not yet printed, Principle lectures.[16]

Logos Litho-Print

A persistent problem faced by all Unified Families was the necessity of economic support. Because nearly all members held full-time jobs, evangelistic activities were curtailed, being limited to evening hours and weekends. One attempt to deal with this problem was the setting up of Family businesses. The Washington Center experimented with "Kim Home Cleaning" and "Omega Office Service." During the 1970 Christmas season, members sold Pixie Chimes, Popcorn Plastic Plaques, and Holiday Sachets door to door at a forty percent commission from the Gattis Corporation, a wholesale notions outfit, to raise funds for the printing of new songbooks.[17]

The Berkeley Center concentrated its business endeavors on printing. Whether in response to Mr. Choi's International Exchange Press in San Francisco or not, by November, 1968, the Berkeley Center acquired an offset printing press and in early 1969 established Logos Litho-Print in a small shop off Telegraph Avenue in Berkeley. From those beginnings, Logos Litho-Print expanded to include a secretarial service, two additional presses, an IBM composer, and a process camera housed in a twenty-one room building with over 7,000 feet of office space.[18]

Student Groups and Koinonia

Most of the Berkeley center's members were students. A January, 1970, report noted that only three of the center's twenty-one members were non-students, and of those three, two were teachers[19] While several members attended the University of California at Berkeley, a June, 1970 report counted members at two local high schools and six area colleges. At least seven members joined from Holy Names College in Oakland.

This development was consistent with the Washington trend toward an active witness on college campuses. There, the center flooded the Washington Area Free University Catalogue with a variety of New Age courses. Standing out among the cooking

and literature classes, listings included The New Man, The End
of the World, Dawn of a New Age, In Search of Freedom, and
The 21st Century.[20] Besides Free University offerings, the
Washington Center launched incipient campus clubs at the
University of Maryland, Georgetown, American University, and
Catholic University.

In Berkeley, this pattern emerged on the University of
California campus in April, 1969, with the establishment of a
new club, the Forum for New Age Unification. The name was
changed to Students for New Age Unification in January, 1970,
and finally to Students for World Unification, (SWU) in 1971 to
be consistent with the Washington group. In that same year,
several Berkeley Center members organized Students for
Integrated Education and offered an accredited course at the
University of California. Entitled "Integrated Education I:
Contemporary Problems," the course was available for four units
of independent study credit through the sociology and economics
departments.[21]

Aside from campus activity, the other educational outlet of
the Unified Family was *Koinonia*. Described in a brochure as
"an opportunity for young adults to interact in dialogue in an
informal atmosphere," *Koinonia* attempted to appeal "to the
serious individual who is interested in participating with others
in a search for deeper understanding."[22] Weekly programs
focused on themes of a religious or philosophical nature and
included outside lecturers, entertainment and refreshments. While
Washington's biggest turnout was twenty-eight non-family
members to hear Dr. Nikolai Khokhlov, a Russian psychologist,
Berkeley *Koinonia* set "an all-time attendance record" of nearly
four hundred people by sponsoring a talk by thirteen-year-old
guru Balyogeshwar Shri Sant Ji Marahaj in August, 1971.
Although this number was impressive, one Berkeley member
complained that many who attended "were not of the best quality
and thus the attempt to use this as a witnessing opportunity was
by and large frustrated."[23]

The Freedom Leadership Foundation

If the Unified Family's business and educational efforts meant more interaction with society, political involvement held forth the same promise. Previously almost apolitical, Miss Kim's group became increasingly active in the late 1960s in order to link up with the movement's anti-communist activities in Japan and Korea. The first step in this linkage was the founding of the Freedom Leadership Foundation (FLF) in the summer of 1969. Conceived of as an educational foundation, FLF held its first workshops for church members in August and September of that year.

Despite opposition from some within the movement, Unified Family centers quickly established FLF affiliates throughout the country. However, activities clearly were focused in Washington. There, FLF President Neil Salonen fashioned a broad coalition with the Student Coordinating Committee for Peace with Freedom in October, 1969. Consciously attempting to preempt the October 15, 1969 antiwar moratorium, more than forty students joined in a three day fast beginning Thursday, October 10. Urging citizens "to take a positive and constructive approach toward a very complex problem, rather than retreating behind a very simplistic, unrealistic solution," the fast attracted wide coverage. FLF President and Fast Coordinator Neil Salonen noted:

> Although we organized on short notice, we were covered by two local television stations each evening and our final rally was broadcast on nationwide NBC television. Most of those fasting were interviewed on radio stations for broadcast during their news programs. In addition, the news of our fast was carried to all newspapers in the country through United Press International (UPI) and Associated Press (AP). Many congressmen sent messages of their support in the days following the fast.[24]

Even more noteworthy was a wire of thanks received from
President Nixon:

> I have noticed your three-day fast for freedom in
> Vietnam and I am grateful for your understanding and
> support of our patient efforts to achieve peace in
> Vietnam with freedom and justice, without which any
> peace could not be durable or endurable.[25]

Undoubtedly, such early successes went a long way toward
silencing internal opposition to political involvement. In this
sense, the real impact of the fast was less on society than on the
movement itself. When FLF acquired Federal tax-exempt status
which prohibited lobbying and demonstrations, members formed
new coalitions. American Youth for a Just Peace (AYJP) was
organized in May, 1970, to lobby in defense of U.S. action in
Cambodia and against the McGovern-Hatfield and
Cooper-Church bills.[26]

The Berkeley Center sent representatives to FLF workshops
and started its own chapter to begin raising the consciousness of
its members about Marxist-Leninist ideology. However, given
the nature of Berkeley, it was not long before
consciousness-raising became confrontational. Even by Berkeley
campus standards, a noticeable flap ensued as a result of AYJP
activities on the campus of the University of California in May,
1971.

Earlier that spring, Neil Salonen traveled to South Vietnam
to obtain from Saigon students groups a refutation of the then
widely publicized People's Peace Treaty. An effort to make
peace among the students of North and South Vietnam and the
United States,treaty supporters claimed the support of the South
Vietnam National Student Union, a supposed 35,000 member
student organization there. Neil Salonen found this to be a
"totally fictitious organization" and AYJP mobilized to counter
"ratification" efforts by students at American colleges.

In Berkeley, a May 12, 1971, Press Conference called by
FLF and AYJP Berkeley chapter President Dan Fefferman

highlighted the confrontational aspects of this effort. With nearly seventy people in attendance, including three Bay Area television news teams and press representatives from the *Daily Californian*, Berkeley *Gazette* and San Francisco *Chronicle*, Fefferman read a statement "exposing" the People's Peace Treaty. Equally significant was his summary of AYJP's stance in Berkeley:

> Our group has been active on campus for about three weeks. The response of the radicals to our presence exposes them for the reactionaries that they are. We have been threatened, physically intimidated, and accused of being CIA agents every day. Our posters have been ripped down, our signs defaced and our sisters insulted.[27]

Rev. Moon's Second World Tour

It is impossible to appreciate the spiritual, economic, educational, and political "full-scale advance" of local centers such as Berkeley without reference to Rev. Moon's thirty-nine day visit to the United States as a part of his second world tour in February and March, 1969. Accompanied by Mrs. Moon, Mr. Eu (President of HSA-UWC, Korea), Mrs. Won Pak Choi, and Mr. Kuboki (President of HSA-UWC, Japan), Rev. Moon arrived at San Francisco International Airport on February 4, 1969 and at Washington headquarters on February 9th. It was during this stay that assembled American members heard first-hand of anti-communist and student activities of the Korean and Japanese members.

Equally significant were Mr. Eu's *Divine Principle* lectures which American members heard for the first time. Finally, Rev. Moon's whirlwind tour of machine shops in New York City raised members' consciousness with regard to economic enterprises.

If these activities were determinative of the four lines of attack already discussed, the major focus of Rev. Moon's stay in

Washington, D.C., was the blessing in marriage of thirteen American couples: six previously married and seven new couples. The first marriage in the church outside of Korea, those taking part in the February 2th ceremony included George Norton and the Pumphreys from Miss Kim's original Bay Area group. Other participants were Edwin Ang from Berkeley, American HSA-UWC President Philip Burley, and two couples from Mr. Kim's Northwest group.[28]

Following Rev. Moon and his party's departure from Kennedy International Airport on March 15, 1969, another wedding for eight couples was held in Essen, Germany, on March 28, 1969. There, Pauline Phillips and Doris Walder from Miss Kim's original Bay Area community were "blessed." Other participants there included Elke Klawiter, Peter Koch, the Werners and Barbara Koch, all of whom had joined under Miss Kim in the Bay Area. A third ceremony for twenty-two couples in Japan was held in late April, 1969.

The impact of Rev. Moon's second world tour on the American church was reflected both in a full scale advance of local centers and in a re-emerged sense of national solidarity and urgency, at least among Miss Kim's group. Spurred on by newly blessed members joining spouses in the field, Washington Center reports began emphasizing the "outgo" of its members in May, 1969. By June, headquarters members had reinforced activities in Berkeley, Toronto (Canada), Philadelphia, New York, Baltimore, St. Louis, and Miami. They had begun new centers in College Park, Maryland, and New Haven, Connecticut. In that same month of June, HSA-UWC President Philip Burley reinstituted monthly Field Operations reports with witnessing results.[29]

Despite these developments, efforts to forge a national movement were abortive. Again, the difficulties were at headquarters center. This time, however, the problem was less a top-heavy national staff than it was the formation of new organizations—FLF, student groups, and *Koinonia*—designed to influence society rather than to convert individuals. This development, when combined with the "outgo" of Washington's best witnessing members, created a situation of immobility at headquarters reminiscent of 1966. Once again, the discrepancy between organizational initiatives and the hard facts of witnessing results produced casualties starting at the top—this time, HSA-UWC President Philip Burley, who resigned in November, 1969, and joined the "outgo" of Washington members by starting a new center in Boston.

Reconsolidation

The Berkeley Center's connection to national headquarters solidified in December, 1969, when Farley Jones replaced Philip Burley as the new president of HSA-UWC and moved to Washington, D.C. Farley, who "played the role of out-front charger-up" in the Berkeley Center, brought the same spirit to Washington. In January, 1970, he initiated a forty-day movement with chain fasts, prayer teams, and "witno-ventures" to bring new members. When Miss Kim left for a visit to Korea in February, he called for a "National 90-Day Prayer Condition" of support. During this period, Washington Center members fasted one day per week, witnessed to at least three people per day, and prayed together for an hour every evening. At the same time, weekend witnessing intensified and six members completed seven day fasts. By April, 1970, in his first quarterly report, Farley announced "the transferral to other centers of four older Washington Center members."[30]

Although these developments were significant, they were overshadowed by news Miss Kim brought back from Korea in June, 1970, of an international marriage of over seven hundred couples to be held in Seoul the following October. Included among the five prospective couples from Miss Kim's group were Farley Jones and Betsy O'Neill. Called the "largest mass wedding in history" and covered by the *Washington Post* and *Time* magazine, the marriage was crucial to the American movement's development as it afforded members first-hand exposure to the Japanese and Korean churches. For several, this exposure was devastating. One wrote:

> In Japan and Korea . . . the time spent with Miss Kim was often difficult for her and for all of us . . . . I am sure that she also hoped we would take greater responsibility than we ever dreamed to attempt to take in re-directing our American movement after the pattern of our far-eastern families. So many times, through her instruction and direction, we were exposed to brutally truthful comparisons between the sacrificial, passionate, deep Japanese and Korean members and ourselves, as individuals and as representatives of our American movement.[31]

The gap was not only attitudinal. It also was evident in concrete accomplishments. In Japan, members arrived in time to participate in the World Anti-Communist League (WACL) conference for which the Japanese church had raised $1,800,000 through a nationwide street solicitation and flower-selling campaign.[32] In Korea, they stayed in a compound consisting of a factory, two dormitories and a lecture hall built by Korean members for economic and anti-communist work.

All of this had great impact on a new plan for American mobilization announced by Farley Jones at the movement's first "Director's Conference" held in Washington from December 31, 1970, to January 3, 1971. In his opening address, Farley stated, "We have never fulfilled the minimum foundation of faith necessary for a strong movement in America,"[33] and in the course of the conference announced two decisive measures: one symbolic and the other practical. First, Miss Kim's group changed its name from the "Unified Family" to the "Unification Church" for the purpose of effecting impact, respectability, and stability. Second, the group altered its organizational thrust from a policy of "unregulated expansionism" to a policy of "reconsolidation" whereby they would consolidate "from twenty-one small groups to five points of power—Berkeley, Denver, Los Angeles, New York, and Washington."[34]

To some extent, the new policy was a Berkeley initiative. Following Farley's speech, Edwin Ang, a chief architect of the reconsolidation plan, outlined arguments in favor of the proposal. Arguing that the American movement should be able to double its membership yearly as that "has been the pattern in general in Berkeley and other centers when they have been spiritually strong," Edwin elaborated a multiplication scheme. According to his figures, expansion from the group's present size "to a movement of some 15,000 persons" (the number he described as minimal in order to have nationwide impact) in the next six years was not an optimistic goal. It was, rather, "what can be done with only an ordinary amount of sacrifice and a more efficient method of training."[35]

Besides membership growth, several other arguments were advanced for acceptance of the proposal. It was suggested that for a small center "to try to carry on vigorous spiritual work, and at the same time make a strong political impression on the community, and start a Family business is not reasonable . . . the Center Director is worn out trying to solve problems in each of the three contexts." The advantages of reconsolidation in alleviating communication breakdowns between headquarters and local centers was also stressed. However, by far the most effective argument for acceptance of sweeping changes was the example of the Japanese and Korean churches, a point that was driven home for conference participants through a presentation of slides from the recent trip. Particularly humiliating was what Farley termed, "the gulf between the accomplishments of the Japanese and ourselves over equal periods of effort." One member wrote:

> Even taking into account the cultural differences and the visits of Our Leader, there is still much that can only be explained by some lack in ourselves.[36]

In short, the feeling was that the American movement had to make bold moves to demonstrate its faith. Although Miss Kim remained in Korea following the October 1970 wedding, Mrs. Shin Wook (Lady Doctor) Kim, an early member and recent immigrant utilized the phrase, "No wet cheeks in America," to indicate a lack of desperation and dependence on God. By pulling up stakes, leaving homes, jobs, and friends, reconsolidation seemed to be a way to demonstrate commitment and to taste tears. Nor were appeals to the American tradition of "rising to the occasion" lacking. As one member stated, "Centuries from now, let us look back, with the thought that the American movement was truly born here, through our energetic implementation of these guidelines."[37]

Unfortunately, these hopes were disappointed. Despite an initial euphoria which cast "caravans" from smaller centers after the fashion of Abraham journeying from Ur of Chaldea or the Israelites traveling to Canaan, there were problems. First, although Farley and Edwin sold the idea of reconsolidation to gathered directors, the directors had to sell the idea to local membership. It was one thing to agree to the proposal *en masse* at headquarters and quite another thing to convince members in the field. That there were compromises is evident in the February/March *New Age Frontiers'* reference to "the huge task of consolidating sixteen centers into eight" as opposed to the original ratio of twenty-one to five. Second, for those centers which did receive substantial reinforcements, such as the Washington Center, which grew from thirty to seventy members in one month, there were serious adjustment problems. A member from Washington, D.C., wrote:

> In this time of transition, we are experiencing many feelings: how will we maintain a strong sense of family relationship in such a large center? How will we survive spiritually in such cramped quarters? What on earth will we do about the hot water situation? We feel lost without personal attention from our leaders—so much more available in the past.[38]

The answer to most of these problems, at least at headquarters, was increased organization. Small committees met with directors "to plan how to effectively use the multiplied energy now available." FLF assembled a full-time staff and a national training program began. However, the new problem was a growing discrepancy between the "leap of faith" that had brought members to Washington and the emergent bureaucracy that greeted them on arrival. Moreover, emphasis had shifted once again from winning converts to influencing society.

This social thrust was evident at the Second National Director's Conference held in Washington beginning June 27, 1971. Taking as its theme, "The Winning of America," Farley's opening address dealt not about the need to establish a foundation of faith but about "the need to widen the scope of our activity . . . by developing new programs and activities." Rather than slides from Korea and Japan, the conference featured a series of films on executive management."[39] A *New Age Frontiers* editorial, evaluating the Second National Director's Conference, contended:

> There was a time in our movement when we truly believed that to build the Kingdom of God in America, we had only to witness every day and teach as many people as possible. . . . Our belief . . . was not misguided, only very childlike.[40]

The new direction was "out of the era of blind faith" and into a sphere of "creative effort." The same editorial spoke of utilizing the experiences of other movements, the patterns "that are working in Korea and Japan," and "with the help of God," fashioning a synthesis "tailored to the American need." However, in seeking to spark "a renaissance of American civilization," this thrust dissipated witnessing energies. Although the dearth of new members was less conspicuous amid crowded conditions, the gaps in the "monthly" *New Age Frontiers* (only two issues between July and December, 1971) pointed to a general lack of activity. By focusing energy on "The Winning of America," the reconsolidation effort lost its cutting edge.

If reconsolidation efforts were blunted on the national level, the Berkeley Center was a good example of the effects of reconsolidation locally. There, the Kansas City group arrived in June, 1971. By August, half of that contingent and their director had returned to Kansas City. A later Berkeley Center "Evaluation of Spiritual Activities, 1971" noted that the influx of large numbers of people created problems of coordinating people and housing, brought a different orientation of Principle, criticism of the established center pattern and confusion over leadership roles. Reconsolidation, in short, was a distraction to the Berkeley Center. It compounded problems rather than benefits. Whereas the center began 1971 with forty members and with a goal to reach eighty by 1972, the actual number at the close of the year was fifty-two.[41]

Equally distressing as the failure to double membership were the conflicts that emerged as a result of the Kansas City split. One leader angrily told those departing that they were not true members, that they could not teach the Principle, and that they would never be blessed (i.e., married) in the church. In this sense, the final upshot of reconsolidation was a painful realization that no less than rival missionary groups, Miss Kim's own group was disunited and splintered.

United Faith, Inc.

The whole time that Miss Kim's group was working to forge a national movement, Mr. David (Sang Chul) Kim's Northwest group continued to be active and a factor on the national scene. "United Faith, Inc.," as the Northwest group was officially known, was also a factor in the Bay Area. Although Mr. Kim's Oakland Chapel did not experience the growth of either Miss Kim's group in Berkeley or Mr. Choi's group in San Francisco, his group's presence in the Bay Area had local and movement-wide ramifications. For this reason, it is important to consider both the Northwest family's Bay Area activities and its relationship to the other missionary groups.

Bay Area activities

Unlike Miss Kim's original group and Mr. Choi's later group, Mr. Kim's Northwest group never thought of the Bay Area as their primary mission field. First and foremost, Mr. Kim was "missionary to the Northwest." Inheriting members that Miss Kim left behind in Eugene and raising his own converts in Portland, a major thrust of the Northwest group from its beginnings were yearly "Forty day evangelical campaigns" of often solitary missionaries traveling as far east as Chicago. By July, 1965, the group's newsletter, *United Temple Bulletin*, claimed six states where "our Northwest families" are working: Chicago, Illinois; Cheyenne, Wyoming; Boise, Idaho; Salt Lake City, Utah; Seattle, Washington; Portland, St. Helens, and Eugene, Oregon.[42] The Bay Area was added to this list on September 1 1965 when Mr. Kim enrolled at Pacific School of Religion in Berkeley.

Living at Edwin Ang's apartment in Berkeley until moving to Oakland in January, 1966, David Kim attended Pacific School of Religion, the second seminary and fourth school he had attended since coming to America in 1959. Unlike Miss Kim who began full-time missionary work five years previously, Mr. Kim was forced to retain his student status in a constant battle to remain in the country. After being expelled from Western Conservative Baptist Seminary in 1961 as a result of damaging testimony from disaffected members who attempted to have him deported, Mr. Kim enrolled at Portland University, the University of Oregon (M.A. in Education, 1965) and Pacific School of Religion in a constant effort to keep ahead of the immigration authorities. As he later wrote,

> I have been under constant persecution and have traveled some mighty thorny roads. It was all I could

do to survive and to remain in this country in order to continue to fulfill my heavenly mission.[43]

Mr. Kim's "heavenly mission" took him to Clearfield, Utah, in September, 1966, after an eight month stint as a rehabilitation counselor intern for Goodwill Industries in the San Francisco Bay Area. Immigration officials had allowed him to retain his student visa while pursuing full-time employment with the Thiokol Chemical Corporation as a counselor for culturally deprived youth at the Clearfield, Utah, Job Corps Center. From his Clearfield base, Mr. Kim directed Northwest family operations for the next five years.

Although David Kim left the Bay Area in September, 1966, the Northwest family remained. In August, the *United Temple Bulletin* reported on witnessing efforts of Mr. Kim and two other Northwest members at the University of California campus, Berkeley. The ranks were further bolstered in July, 1966, by the arrival from Korea of David Kim's wife and youngest son. Because of Mr. Kim's visa status, his immediate family was required to maintain residency in California. In this way, a nucleus of Northwest members remained for the duration of David Kim's Job Corps tour.

A new stage of Northwest involvement in the Bay Area began following incorporation of the group as United Faith, Inc. in June, 1969. The previous October, through the intercessory efforts of Congressman Lawrence J. Burton (R-Utah), David Kim won his immigration battle and was awarded a permanent visa.[44] Covered fairly substantially by Utah news media as a human interest story, this victory as well as the May, 1969 arrival in Oakland of David Kim's three college aged sons helped point the Northwest movement in new directions.

More important, however, was Rev. Moon's second world tour. Just as with Miss Kim's group, the impact of Rev. Moon's 1969 visit on Northwest members (four of whom were blessed in Washington, D.C.) was that of revitalization and expanded vision. In the Northwest group, this took the form of a massive reorganization. On June 12, 1969, Mr. Kim and his eldest son,

Sung Soo, traveled to Portland, Oregon to attend a Northwest
Board of Directors meeting. There, as reported in the *United
Temple Bulletin*, "In order to advance our United Faith
Movement to an international level, the name of 'United Chapel
of Portland, Inc.' was changed to 'United Faith, Inc.'" Part of
this reorganization also included the appointment of directors,
assistant directors, and committee members for departments of
Administrative Affairs, Home and Foreign Missions,
International Cultural Exchange, and Enterprise.[45]

As a result of David Kim gaining his permanent visa,
favorable publicity in the Utah press, Rev. Moon's visit, the
arrival of Mr. Kim's three sons, and the reorganization of the
Northwest movement, a feeling of optimism prevailed within the
ranks of United Faith, Inc., during the summer and autumn of
1969. In October, David Kim asserted, "Spiritually our N.W.
family work will grow from now on." In November, he stated,

> We already set up our permanent Structure (Four
> Departments) under the new name of our organization
> (United Faith, Inc.), and responsible personnel are
> appointed. From now on the rest of the task is to wait
> and see how the system works and how each of us as
> strong Heavenly Soldiers can function and fulfill our
> missions in each state.[46]

In short, the system didn't work. Mr. Kim instructed that
"each member bring 3 converts," but by the end of 1969 the
heavenly soldiers were themselves struggling. "The month of
December," as Mr. Kim noted, had "been very low for all
families in the Northwest." There were serious financial
problems and physical illness. Moreover, caught in the crunch
between organizational initiatives and a general lack of concrete
results, there were casualties.

The most drastic of these casualties was the Berkeley Chapel.
There, several Bay Area married couples as well as a "United
Barber Shop" of Alameda (two barbers converted) had loosely
affiliated themselves in a weekly fellowship but found the

pressures of maintaining a chapel too much for them. Thus, despite a solemn November 9, 1969, dedication ceremony and a proclamation "to Heaven and Earth," the newly established Berkeley chapel (1104 Shattuck Avenue) all but folded in January, 1970. In February, Mr. Kim was asking for "prayers to restore the Berkeley chapel financially and membership-wise." By March, he was forced to note, "The situation of the Bay Area in relation to the Berkeley family problem has been getting worse . . . almost at the verge of total failure."[47]

The final stage of Northwest activities in the Bay Area followed David Kim's resignation from the Job Corps and his return to Oakland in February, 1971. The previous August he had returned to Korea for a ten day visit (his first since coming to America in 1959) and, like Miss Kim and her members, was impressed with activities there, especially the anti-communist work. While in Korea, he was asked by Rev. Moon when he would be ready for reassignment, and a Buddhist spiritualist prophesied of his coming "Heavenly Mission" after "long suffering and long preparation of 10 years."[48] All of these encounters were influential on Mr. Kim's decision to leave the Job Corps. In December 1970 he wrote:

> I am seriously thinking of my resignation from the job to engage myself in full-time missionary work and to launch Anti-Communist campaigns. . . . Many unsettled problems I have, personally and financially, etc. But I can not let my time run out.[49]

Following a December 28, 1970, Board of Directors Meeting at the Utah Chapel, at which time United Faith, Inc. representatives were re-appointed to ten states and Canada, Mr. Kim, on January 4, 1971, submitted his resignation to the Clearfield Job Corps Center, giving thirty days notice. As he stated in his resignation paper, "My future plans are to engage more actively in so-called 'United Faith Movement' on the international level from the month of February, 1971."[50] Mr. Kim's wife came to Utah to accompany him to California, and on February 14, they left, arriving at Oakland on February 15, 1971. Mr. Kim wrote:

> I am now on a new mission field, Bay Area in California after I spent 5 years in Utah, and I joined my immediate family after long years separation. [51]

Although Mr. Kim had hopes of reviving the Bay Area situation and on the day after his arrival "visited all old members in Oakland and Berkeley," he found little response. Apart from his immediate family, for whom he organized a weekly "English Principle Study Hour," his only stalwart follower in the Bay Area was sixty-three year old John Schmidli, Mr. Kim's first convert in America. Although "Uncle" John witnessed daily, the Northwest family was not about to challenge either the Berkeley Center or Mr. Choi's Re-Education Foundation in gaining new members. For this reason, Mr. Kim moved in another direction.

During his visit to Korea and during a two-day stopover in Japan, Mr. Kim spent much of his time collecting written materials and conversing with officials of the movement's "International Federation for Victory Over Communism" (IFVC). He also spent an entire night in conversation with Dr. Sang Hun Lee, a medical doctor and author of IFVC's basic text. After his return to the Bay Area, Mr. Kim's most consuming task was the translation of Dr. Lee's *New Critique on Communism*.

Assisted by several local members, Mr. Kim completed his handwritten manuscript, *Victory Over Communism and the Role of Religion*, on May 1, 1971, and dedicated it at Twin Peaks, San Francisco. By July, twelve typed copies of the manuscript were sent to key Northwest family members for their intensive study. Perhaps, anticipating the problems attending earlier translations of the *Principle*, Mr. Kim sent a copy of the manuscript to Dr. Lee and noted, "He is very pleased to see his original writing translated exactly into English." In October, Mr. Kim announced that a contract had been made with publishers. In his words,

Hopefully before this year is over all will be completed and in early spring national and international markets shall have our books—not only in U.S. and Canada but even in Europe—arousing much public opinion.[52]

Relationship with other groups

Just as important as the Northwest group's own activities was its relationship to the other missionary groups. Part of that relationship was referred to earlier in the *United Temple Bulletin*'s May, 1966, "Expressed Opinions on so called 'National Headquarters' in Washington, D.C., by the Northwest Families." At that time, following Rev. Moon's 1965 world tour, David Kim and Mr. Choi joined forces in the Bay Area to counter Miss Kim's national thrust in Washington, D.C. However, following Rev. Moon's second world tour in 1969, Mr. Kim moved toward Miss Kim's group (particularly Edwin Ang's Berkeley Center) in an effort to counter the influence of Mr. Choi's International Re-Education Foundation.

To understand this shift as well as its Bay Area and movement-wide ramifications, it is necessary to develop more fully Mr. Kim's Northwest group's relationship to Miss Kim's and Mr. Choi's groups following Rev. Moon's 1965 and 1969 world tours.

Post 1965. Following Rev. Moon's first world tour, in October, 1965, the United States was divided into four missionary jurisdictions: San Francisco for Miss Kim; the Northwest for Mr. Kim; Chicago for Mr. Choi; and Washington, D.C., for Col. Pak. Although this arrangement was authorized by Rev. Moon, the jurisdictions were undermined by two developments in December, 1965. First, as a result of career obligations and increasing involvement with his newly formed Korean Cultural and Freedom Foundation (KCFF), Col. Bo Hi Pak found it impossible to continue full-time missionary work, and Miss Kim moved to Washington, D.C. Second, as a result of Miss Kim's departure, his own delicate health and Mr. Kim's urging, Mr. Choi remained in the Bay Area. While this new lineup of Miss Kim and Bo Hi Pak in the East and Mr. Kim and Mr. Choi in the West was clearly the result of unforeseen circumstances and confessedly provisional, the original fourfold jurisdiction was never realized. The result was an East-West tension that riddled all attempts to forge a national movement in the 1960s.

In a very real sense, David Kim and Mr. Choi were tossed into one another's arms following Rev. Moon's 1965 tour. Not only did Mr. Choi live with Mr. Kim at Edwin Ang's Berkeley apartment for the first month and a half after his arrival, but also following Mr. Choi's move to San Francisco and Mr. Kim's move to Oakland, they continued to join together for witnessing, holidays, and worship services. More important they joined together in attempting to form a West Coast coalition to combat Miss Kim's national headquarters in Washington, D.C.

The dimensions of this West Coast coalition were first evident at the third Northwest "Monthly Training Conference" in Portland, Oregon, March 19-21, 1966. Although Edwin Ang was conspicuously absent, Mr. Choi and five members of the "Japanese" family from San Francisco, Lowell Martin from Oakland, and John Pinkerton, director of the Los Angeles Center all attended. The following month, while Miss Kim was touring East Coast centers, Mr. Kim was in Los Angeles showing slides of Bay Area activities and conducting Sunday service. Finally, in May, 1966, the same month that "Expressed Opinions on so called National Headquarters. . ." was published in the *United Temple Bulletin*, an "executive committee of the Bay Area" was formed consisting of the two Korean missionaries and three local members. Rather than centralization, the committee stressed local autonomy in witnessing and center activities.[53]

The culmination of this West Coast coalition came at a May 28-30, 1966, "United West Coast Fellowship" in Oakland. There, over forty people gathered, representing ten centers from Anchorage, Alaska, to Los Angeles, California. Weekend activities included general introductions, reports, sample lectures and impromptu fellowship. On Sunday, Mr. Choi spoke for one and one half hours in the morning and Mr. Kim for two hours in the afternoon. The final one and one half hour of the afternoon was taken by Col. Bo Hi Pak, an unexpected guest from Washington, D.C. Not surprisingly, his presence was disruptive. According to a Northwest member,

> He spoke on the absolute seriousness of our work and then on "Unity." This topic broke our weekend atmosphere of fellowship. It was previously agreed that we would not have a group discussion on this matter of unity until a future date, and then with *only* major parties involved. Because our fellowship atmosphere was destroyed we spent only a short time sharing songs with our Japanese brothers and sisters. Then we left early.[54]

Although Col. Pak broke the fellowship atmosphere, he succeeded in drawing a number of Miss Kim's West Coast members back into the Washington fold. On the other hand, Mr. Kim's and Mr. Choi's groups drew closer together. These ties were cemented further when Mr. Kim's wife and youngest son arrived in the Bay Area, June 24, 1966. Not only were Mrs. Kim and Mrs. Choi old friends but Mrs. Kim brought direct tidings from Rev. Moon that he was "very pleased that Mr. Kim and Mr. Nishikawa (Mr. Choi) are working together in the San Francisco area . . . that Mr. Kim should stand on the position he has taken on the matter of unity, and that he will straighten out all things when he comes to America."[55] Although David Kim left for Clearfield, Utah, in early September, 1966, the East-West missionary division was officially recognized by Rev. Moon in an October 2, 1966, letter to Mr. Choi. Mr. Choi was officially reassigned to stay in San Francisco, and further discussion on the problem of uniting with Washington, D.C., was prohibited. A letter with the same content was sent to Jim Fleming in Washington, D.C.

Post 1969. During Rev. Moon's 1969 world tour, the East-West jurisdictional division was clarified at a ten-hour missionary conference at Washington, D.C., on February 22, 1969. As reported in the *United Temple Bulletin*,

> This misunderstandings and conflicts of the 3 groups were clarified and called for mutual respect and cooperation among the 3 groups in the U.S. from now on. Our Master announced the U.S. would be divided into 2 missionary jurisdictions—the West and the East. San Francisco will be the headquarters which will be supervised by Mr. Choi, while Washington, D.C., will be supervised by Miss Kim, and Mr. David Kim will be assigned later for new responsibility. In the meantime, he will assist Mr. Choi in being responsible for the West.[56]

Despite these clarifications, problems persisted. The renewed "outgo" and initiatives of Washington, D.C., headquarters following Rev. Moon's departure again impinged on Northwest operations. In July, 1969, the *United Temple Bulletin* published a June 15 "Letter to Our Master on the Long Existing Conflicts Between West and East Groups." Included among the by now familiar litany of charges were the following:

a. Constant conflicts with Washington group instead of harmony and mutual cooperation.
b. Constantly trying to dominate the N.W. group by Washington group members.
c. Taking away members from other groups to Washington, D.C., group (sending a worker to Oregon City, 20 miles from Portland, Oregon, chapel, to separate members from us.
d. Slandering and insulting Mr. David Kim—making propaganda that David Kim is resigned from his missionary work and that he no longer controls and supervises the Northwest and the West Coast, etc.

   e. Requesting all kinds of monthly reports from other groups and asking for contributions to Washington, D.C. by blessed couples. But we have lots of doubt on their use of these funds.

   f. Openly making propaganda that Miss Kim's translation of the Principle is the only legitimate text approved by our Master and that Mr. David Kim's translation is not approved even if it is the exact translation of Mr Rhyu's [Hyo Won Eu] lecture series in Korean.[57]

To counter Washington, D.C., initiatives, the Northwest family established "United Faith, Inc." in June, 1969. Mr. Kim wrote to his membership:

> By my systematic observation there are long years to go to be U.S. Headquarters, even after I recently visited Washington, D.C. in February, 1969. So do your part and fulfill your Heavenly responsibility in America. Don't be upset. I will be with you as your teacher, adviser, counselor and your Korean missionary sent directly by our Master. From now on march on with your new organization—United Faith, Inc. You have an independent organization different from Mr. Choi's or Miss Kim's.[58]

Significant here was Mr. Kim's assertion of independence from Mr. Choi's as well as from Miss Kim's group. Likewise, in a November, 1969, report, Mr. Kim noted, "In S.F. Bay Area two other groups besides ours are working—Mr. Choi, Miss Kim's group—in future we will work together as a team, but the time is not ripe yet."[59] In this sense, establishment of United Faith, Inc., signalled the initial move of Mr. Kim's group away from Mr. Choi. This trend was more dramatic following David Kim's 1971 return to the Bay Area. Not only did he continue to move away from Mr. Choi, but he began to move toward Miss Kim's group, particularly Edwin Ang's Berkeley Center, in an effort to counter Mr. Choi's influence in San Francisco. To understand this surprising reversal, it is necessary to highlight three separate developments: controversy over marketing a sports air gun, the anti-communist movement, and the growth of Mr. Choi's group.

Following the February, 1969, missionary conference, Rev. Moon spoke of selling a sports air gun in the United States. Invented by a Korean church member and manufactured at the movement's Sootaek-Ri factory compound outside Seoul, the suggestion was controversial. Both Miss Kim and Mr. Choi, whose groups were self-supporting, expressed concern about the effects of gun sales on their public image. On the other hand, David Kim's group, with less to lose, was more supportive. While Mr. Kim's position on the Sports Air Gun had not drawn him any closer to Miss Kim, it did create an initial chink in his relationship with Mr. Choi.

If David Kim's position on marketing a sports air gun created an initial chink in his relationship with Mr. Choi, his enthusiastic support of the church's anti-communist movement drew him closer to Miss Kim's group. Here, Mr. Kim's interests meshed with Freedom Leadership Foundation (FLF) activities and made for significant breakthroughs. On April 19, 1971, FLF President Neil Salonen visited the Oakland chapel on his return from South Vietnam and Korea. The following month, Mr. Kim was in attendance at the Press Conference called by Berkeley "American Youth for a Just Peace" (AYJP) chapter president, Dan Fefferman."[60]

The most significant breakthrough involved a rapprochement between David Kim and Washington, D.C., Headquarters. Traveling there in late June, 1971, to attend an "antisubversive" seminar conducted by Dr. Fred Schwartz, founder of the Christian Anti-Communist Crusade, Mr. Kim met Miss Kim, Farley Jones (John Farley as Mr. Kim called him), and Neil Salonen. Not only was Mr. Kim impressed with FLF's biweekly newsletter, its full-time staff and Washington contacts, but also he was impressed with the headquarters center. He wrote,

I had a chance to dine with all of Washington, D.C., family and I was very much impressed with many enthusiastic faces of college students as well as old members in the center, and I noticed constant progress made in training members, new programs and church activities, and so on.[61]

Again, if the anti-communist movement served to bring Mr. Kim closer to Miss Kim's group, it further alienated him from Mr. Choi, for whom the conflictual elements of an anti-communist crusade simply were not appropriate. For Mr. Choi, communism and capitalism were both wrong, if not irrelevant. What the world needed was an international ideal city built on conscientious common sense.

Although the anticommunist movement was an important factor in Mr. Kim's movement toward Miss Kim's group, an even more important factor was the growth of Mr. Choi's group. Whereas Mr. Choi's "Japanese" family seemed harmless enough in 1966, his "International Re-Education Foundation" appeared ominous by 1971. Particularly threatening was the foundation's emphasis on the "Principles of Education." Edwin Ang, who originally moved to San Francisco with Mr. Choi, broke early to teach the "straight" Principle in Berkeley. He and the Berkeley Center looked askance at the "horizontal" social programming of Mr. Choi's Re-Education Foundation. For their part, Mr. Choi's members viewed the Berkeley Center as "not very highly evolved." For this reason, there had been little, if any, communication between the two groups since 1966.

Following David Kim's return to the Bay Area in February, 1971, his move away from Mr. Choi and toward Miss Kim was evident as he began, on occasion, to join in Berkeley Center activities. In addition, Mr. Kim initiated a Bay Area "Blessed" couples association that met on the first day of each month according to the lunar calendar. On April 25, 1971, four of these couples met at Edwin Ang's place where they "discussed the San Francisco situation in case that Mr. Choi and his wife intend to do their work independently from Hq. Seoul, Korea. . . ."[62]

This suspicion was more serious than all of the charges Mr. Kim's group had leveled at Miss Kim. Rather than his methods, Mr. Choi's loyalty was being questioned.

In any case, David Kim's move was complete. He sided with the Berkeley Center. This new alignment was solidified in August, 1971, when Miss Kim visited the Bay Area to "chat" with Mr. Kim about Rev. Moon's third world tour and West Coast reception. According to Mr. Kim, "She left all to me and Edwin Ang."[63]

Despite all the political posturing, the bottom line of divisions in the American church from 1966 to 1971 went beyond politics to personality. Attempts to forge a national movement during this period were abortive less as a result of political infighting among the missionary groups than as a result of the divergent personal styles of their leaders. Hence, it is impossible to understand either the movement's Bay Area or national development during this period without reference to the biographies of Miss Kim, Mr. Choi, and David Kim. Divisions in the American church were rooted in their life histories.

The backgrounds of Miss Kim and Mr. Choi have been discussed. Miss Kim was an associate professor of religion with an interest in metaphysics and spiritualism. Mr. Choi was a Holiness minister with an interest in social reform. Mr. Kim, on the other hand, had been a government official with an interest in unification of the world's religions. In an account of his background, he wrote:

> Uppermost in my mind was always my concern and special interest in religion, and I continued to study and research religious matters unceasingly. Although I was serving as a deacon and choir director at one of the Presbyterian churches located in Kunsan City, and also was holding the position of National Disbursing Officer of Ministry of Finance, socially, I was daydreaming of uniting the established Christian and Buddhist religions, gathering many faithful friends in order to discuss my ideas on religion. . . . Many religious persons from

Confucianism, Buddhism and Christianity, as well as other small devoted religious groups from the mountains—Buddhist priests, spiritually-gifted individuals, astrologers, physiognomists, etc.—visited me privately all the time. At that time my idea was to re-formulate a new religious structure, incorporating the good points of other religions based on Christianity, and I freely discussed this with my close friends from the Presbyterian church at which I served.[64]

No less than Miss Kim or Mr. Choi for their groups, Mr. Kim shaped the character of the Northwest Family. Thus, rather than as a "church" or as an "educational foundation," Mr. Kim's group consistently identified itself as a "United Faith Movement."[65] For Mr. Kim, the "principles" were cast less in a metaphysical or utopian than in an ecumenical light.

As a result of competing ideas about the nature and purposes of their organizations, differing interpretations of the Principle, and conflicting mission styles, a national movement had not emerged by the end of 1971. Instead, what emerged was a complicated set of missionary jurisdictions, political alliances, and general grievances—nowhere more focused than in the Bay Area. The impasse there was symptomatic of the American movement as a whole.

At the same time, there had been significant developments during the period. Most important were the moves beyond evangelistic witness into economic, cultural, and political activities. This full scale advance continued, though in markedly different fashion following Rev. Moon's third world tour. That tour, begun in late November, 1971, not only inaugurated a unified American movement but also radically restructured priorities. As one of Mr. Choi's Re-Education members wrote, "I sensed some heavy changes were coming."[66]

NOTES

1. Bill Smith, "Report from New York, New York," *New Age Frontiers*, February 1966.

2. Young Oon Kim, "Message for 1966," *New Age Frontiers*, January 1966.

3. "Expressed Opinions on So Called 'National Headquarters,' Washington, D.C., by the Northwest Families," *United Temple Bulletin*, May 1, 1966.

4. Ibid.

5. Ibid.

6. Ibid.

7. Myrtle Hurd, "Report from Washington, D.C.," *New Age Frontiers*, November 1966.

8. Sylvia Rogndahl, "Report from New York City, New York," *New Age Frontiers*, December 1966.

9. Young Oon Kim, "Brightly Beams . . . Washington Family," *New Age Frontiers*, January 1968.

10. Edwin Ang, "Looking Ahead. . ." *New Age Frontiers*, June 1970.

11. Edwin Ang, "Report from Berkeley," *New Age Frontiers*, January 1966.

12. Mr. & Mrs. Farley Jones, "Field Work: Lecture at Unification Theological Seminary," February 23, 1978, unpublished transcript of talk.

13. Jeff Tallakson, "Report from Berkeley," *New Age Frontiers*, February 1969.

14. Vivien and Philip Burley, "Family Department," *New Age Frontiers*, June 1969.

15. Helen Ireland, "Report from Berkeley," *New Age Frontiers*, August 1969.

16. Jeff Tallakson, "Center Life in Berkeley Unified Family," *New Age Frontiers*, June 1970.

17. Sandy Singleton, "Center News Notes," *New Age Frontiers*, January 1971.

18. Felice Walton, "Logos Litho-Print: Berkeley Family Business Grows Up," *New Age Frontiers*, Fall 1971.

19. Jeff Tallakson, "Report from Berkeley," *New Age Frontiers* January 1970.

20. Nora Martin, "Field Operations," *New Age Frontiers*, November 1969.

21. Sandy Singleton, "New Age News," *New Age Frontiers*, May 1971.

22. Nora Martin, "Koinonia—A New Phase," *New Age Frontiers*, February 1970.

23. "New Age News," *New Age Frontiers*, July-August 1971.

24. Neil Albert Salonen, "Student Fast for Freedom," *New Age Frontiers,* November 1969.

25. Ibid.

26. Neil Salonen and Regis Hanna, "Where Does FLF Go from Here?" *New Age Frontiers*, April 1971 and Alan Tate Wood, "What I Learned from the True Parent (My Four and a Half Years with the Lord of the Flies)," January 1, 1976, unpublished manuscript.

27. Dan Fefferman, "Statement to the Press and T.V. Stations," *United Temple Bulletin*, June 1, 1971.

28. Hillie Smith, "Report from Washington, D.C.," *New Age Frontiers,* March 1969.

29. Philip Burley, "Family Department," *New Age Frontiers*, June 1969.

30. Farley Jones, "Quarterly Report," *New Age Frontiers*, April 1970.

31. Hillie Edwards, "In a Time of Crisis, What Is the Pattern of True Individuality?" *New Age Frontiers*, January 1971.

32. "Master Speaks," January 12, 1972, at the Euclid Avenue House, Berkeley, California, unpublished transcript of questions and answers.

33. Regis Hanna, "Editorial," *New Age Frontiers*, January 1971.

34. Sandy Singleton, "Center News Notes," *New Age Frontiers*, January 1971

35. Regis Hanna, "Report on Director's Conference," *New Age Frontiers* January 1971.

36. Ibid.

37. Regis Hanna, "Editorial," *New Age Frontiers*, January 1971.

38. Hillie Edwards, "In a Time of Crisis, What Is the Pattern of True Individuality?" *New Age Frontiers*, January 1971

39. Regis Hanna, "Report on National Director's Conference," *New Age Frontiers*, June, 1971

40. Regis Hanna, "Focus for the Month," *New Age Frontiers*, June 1971.

41. "Evaluation of Spiritual Activities 1971." Unpublished report on the Berkeley center.

42. "Let's Stand by Ourselves," *United Temple Bulletin*, July 1, 1965.

43. David S.C. Kim, "The Establishment of HSA and My Role as One of the Original Participants," *United Temple Bulletin*, May 1970.

44. "News Release from Clearfield Job Corps Training Center, October 3, 1969, 'Utahan to Be Reunited with Family After 5 Years,'" quoted in *United Temple Bulletin*, October 15, 1968.

45. Vernon and Maxine Pearson, "Appointment of Department Directors Under New Organization," *United Temple Bulletin*, June 15, 1966.

46. David S.C. Kim, "News Reports: Clearfield, Utah," *United Temple Bulletin*, October 1969.

47. See *United Temple Bulletin*, November 1969 to March 1970.

48. David S.C. Kim, "News Report", *United Temple Bulletin*, September 1970.

49. David S.C.Kim "News Report" United Temple Bulletin, December 1970.

50. David S.C. Kim, "News Reports: Layton, Utah," *United Temple Bulletin*, February 1971.

51. David S.C. Kim, "News Reports: Oakland, California," *United Temple Bulletin*, March 1971.

52. David S.C. Kim "News Report: Oakland, California," *United Temple Bulletin,* April, August and October 1971.

53. "Brief News Reels: Oakland, California," *United Temple Bulletin*, May 15, 1966.

54. Dianne Pitts, "United West Coast Fellowship," *United Temple Bulletin*, June 1966.

55. "Special News from San Francisco, California," *United Temple Bulletin*, July 1966.

56. David S.C. Kim, "Report on Korean Missionary Conference in Washington, D.C.," *United Temple Bulletin*, March 1969.

57. "Letter to Our Master on the Long-Existing Conflict Between East and West Groups," *United Temple Bulletin*, July 15, 1969.

58. Ibid.

59. David S.C. Kim, "News Report: Clearfield, Utah," *United Temple Bulletin*, November , 1969.

60. "Anti-Marxism Movement Initiated in the West at Berkeley, California, During Month of May," *United Temple Bulletin*, June 1971.

61. David S.C. Kim, "News: Oakland, California," *United Temple Bulletin*, July 1971.

62. David S.C. Kim, "News: Oakland, California," *United Temple Bulletin*, May 1971.

63. David S.C. Kim, "News: Oakland, California," *United Temple Bulletin*, May 1971.

64. David S.C. Kim, "The Establishment of HSA and My Role as One of the Original Participants," *United Temple Bulletin*, May, 1970.

65. "Declaration of the United Faith," *United Temple Bulletin*, August 1963.

66. Kevin Brennan, "When and After Kevin Brennan First Met the Unified Family," Unpublished diary.

CHAPTER SIX

A NATIONAL MOVEMENT EMERGES: 1972-74

The Third World Tour—One World Crusade—Mobile Fundraising Teams—First ICUS Conference—Meeting the Politicos—A National Movement Emerges—Madison Square Garden—The Time Bomb Is Ticking—Success in San Francisco—The Oakland Family

During the years 1972-74, the Unification Church emerged as a national movement in America. Not only had the rival missionary groups merged by the end of this period, but national membership multiplied ten times, evangelistic crusades were held in all fifty states, substantial properties were purchased, international conferences held, and a controversial "Answer to Watergate" statement circulated in full-page advertisements bought from most of the nation's major newspapers. Yet by the end of this period, a good portion of this visibility had turned to notoriety as the movement's rapid growth provoked negative reactions. Questions about the person of Rev. Moon and the teachings of the church surfaced in fundamentalist Christian literature. Questions about the church's aggressive proselytizing, financial backing, organizational objectives, and political ambitions surfaced in secular media accounts. Increasingly, these queries led to organized efforts to stop the movement.

The church in the San Francisco Bay Area was intimately involved in all these developments. Not only were Mr. Choi's

Re-Education Foundation, Miss Kim's Berkeley Center, and Mr. Kim's Oakland chapel non-extant by the end of the period, but virtually all of their members had been moved from the Bay Area to other missions within the movement's national structure. Thus, the impasse among the three missionary groups was no longer an issue, and the way was opened for fresh developments. At the same time, local developments now unfolded within the context of a national movement. Basically, this meant increased public scrutiny. Questions about the movement's religious and organizational legitimacy would become a continuing legacy.

Prior to questions of legitimacy, it is important to understand, as one long time observer later put it, "how a small, faltering and obscure movement of the 1960s was able to achieve rapid growth, stability and prominence in the 1970s."[1] Basically, this development was the result of the movement's organizational initiatives, the conditions of American national life, and the presence of Rev. Moon.

In terms of organizational initiatives, the three-year period 1972-74 divides into two eighteen month phases. The first phase, beginning January 1972, focused on the attainment of internal solidarity. Consisting of a series of 'pioneer' training programs, this phase culminated in the achievement of a viable national structure in all fifty states by July, 1973. The second phase, building on this national network of support, focused on the attainment of public visibility. A succession of evangelistic crusades, this phase culminated in a full house at New York's Madison Square Garden and a triumphant eight-city tour concluding in San Francisco and Los Angeles in December,1974.

Besides organizational initiatives, conditions of American national life fostered the emergence of the Unification Church as a national movement in the 1970s. On the one hand, alienated youth disillusioned both with American society and with the countercultural alternatives of the 1960s enhanced membership and solidarity. On the other hand, live issues, particularly the Watergate crisis, afforded the movement opportunities for national exposure.

While organizational initiatives and the conditions of American national life were significant, of far more importance for the emergence of the Unification Church as a national movement was the unifying and energizing presence of Rev. Moon. If Miss Kim, Mr. Choi, and Mr. Kim all shaped the character of their groups, Rev. Moon gave substance to the national movement. In this sense, it is appropriate to date the birth of the Unification Church of America from his arrival.

The Third World Tour

During Rev. Moon's 1969 world tour, he met with Miss Kim, Mr. Choi, and David Kim, reportedly, "to straighten out the problems of existing conflicts and to set up new missionary jurisdiction until unity of 3 groups takes place in the future when he comes back the third time to the United States."[2] In late 1971, Rev. Moon returned to the United States as part of his third world tour. Accompanied by Mrs. Moon, Mrs. Won Pak Choi, Mr. Young Whi Kim (President, HSA-UWC, Korea since Mr. Eu's death in 1970), and Mr. Ishii (Director, HSA-UWC Business Enterprises, Japan), the party arrived in Los Angeles, December 11, 1971. Denied United States visas, ironically because of alleged communist affiliations, the group flew to Toronto, Canada, the following day. As a result of efforts of the three missionary groups and their contacts, the situation was clarified, and Rev. Moon was granted visa clearance extending until March 14, 1972. On December 18, 1971, he arrived in Washington, D.C.

Speaking to members almost every night from December 21st through the 30th, Rev. Moon requested that Mr. Choi and David Kim attend the movement's God's Day (New Year's) celebration in Washington, D.C., on January 1, 1972. Prior to that, members from Washington, D.C., New York City, Philadelphia, Baltimore, Denver, Berkeley, and St. Louis had assembled for a four-day training program extending from

Friday, December 31 until Monday, January 3. Conducted by
Mr. Young Whi Kim, who "taught the Principle as it is taught
in Korea," it was out of that weekend that what later became
known as "The Plan" emerged.

The Plan

The Plan, as reported in Miss Kim's *New Age Frontiers*, was
"to hold revival meetings in seven major cities—New York,
Philadelphia, Baltimore, Washington, D.C., Los Angeles, San
Francisco, and Berkeley."[3] While Rev. Moon indicated his
desire to hold public meetings on his arrival in Los Angeles, it
was not until the four-day training program that The Plan was
activated, and on January 4, 1972, a joint meeting was held with
East and West Coast leaders to launch the movement's first
national campaign. As Rev. Moon had never spoken publicly
either in Korea or Japan, the birth of the American movement
coincided with the beginning of a new phase in his public
ministry.

Following the joint meeting, further details were announced.
Both East and West Coast centers were to select members,
seventy-two in all, who were to come to New York for a
two-week training session. From there, they would travel from
city to city to hold the revival meetings. After the campaign,
fifty state representatives were to be produced from that group
with the remainder traveling on mobile evangelical bus teams.
Two buses were to make continual evangelical trips to all fifty
states for twelve months, so that each state would have two
revival meetings by two mobile team buses. In addition, five
itinerary workers were to assist the new field centers for one
year. The goal was for 150 new members in each state by the
end of 1972.

While membership goals were important, the primary
objective of the revival meeting period was the attainment of
solidarity within the ranks. The Plan required not only individual
commitment but also cooperation among missionaries, existing

centers, bus teams, newly appointed state representatives, and itinerary workers. As David Kim put it, "This time, all groups will work together to expand our Principle Movement centering in existing chapels, centers, churches, and their members."[4] Leaving little to chance, Rev. Moon announced that personnel from all three groups would be transferred to other places and a rotation system enforced. In any case, the seven-city tour was the first project ever carried out by the national movement.

Implementing The Plan

If The Plan was clear enough, it awaited implementation. Not only did pioneers have to be selected and trained, but a revival meeting itinerary had to be arranged, halls rented, a program set up, posters made, tickets printed and buses purchased. Later state representatives had to be selected and assigned, bus teams formed and itinerary workers appointed. Centering on the seven-city tour, implementation of The Plan included preparations, the tour itself, and the tour's aftermath.

The first step of preparation for the tour was the selection of pioneers for the two-week training session scheduled to begin in New York City on January 14, 1972. On January 9, Rev. Moon, Mrs. Moon, Mrs. Won Pak Choi, and David Kim flew to the San Francisco Bay Area for consultation with Mr. Choi who, in David Kim's words, "returned from the Korean Missionary Conference at D.C. on God's Day, but still had many things to readjust to the new development of our Principle Movement in the U.S." While in the Bay Area, Rev. Moon also visited the Berkeley Center. Although Mr. Choi's Re-Education Foundation contributed fifteen pioneers and the Berkeley Center thirteen, of more significance was the coming together of the two groups on January 11, 1972. As reported in Miss Kim's *New Age Frontiers*, "That night, history was made as the San Francisco and Berkeley Families came together at the Re-Education Center to share a meal and to hear our leader speak."[5]

Prior to traveling to the Bay Area, Rev. Moon journeyed from Washington, D.C. to New York City. There, he rented the Lincoln Center for three nights (February 3-5, 1972) for $3,500 and charged the local center with making plans for the first of seven revival meetings. By January 8th, the New York center had chosen its theme, "The Day of Hope: The Day of the True Family," designed what would be the tour's official poster, and set about finding a church to rent for the pioneer training program.

On January 14, 1972, the pioneers arrived. Housed in the three-story, stone and stucco Bronx center (where previously twenty to thirty New York members had lived in the legally zoned one-family dwelling), seventy-two pioneers and staff traveled daily to St. Steven's Methodist Episcopal Church, where they were accommodated more comfortably for meals and lectures in the basement social hall. The training session focused on building solidarity, a difficult task, given the factions which had developed in the American church. One pioneer wrote:

> There are about eighty of us. We come from different centers throughout the United States. We didn't know each other when we first started. Each of us had different songs, different ways of praying, and different ways of applying the Principle. It was hard to unify at first. But we knew it was necessary.[6]

Unity became increasingly necessary as the opening revival date drew nearer. With less than three weeks to go, training moved from St. Steven's Church to the streets of New York City. One pioneer described the sequence:

> Things started out leisurely enough—breakfast at 8:30, lectures till noon, ticket sales in the afternoon, and more lectures in the evening. Breakfast was soon changed to 6:30 to allow an earlier start. A week later, Master changed the schedule to emphasize ticket sales. We went out to spend eight to ten hours on the streets

> of New York. We returned to St. Steven's at 7:30 or
> 10:00 PM, depending on whether or not we had sold a
> ticket before 6:30.We progressed from four to ten
> hours a day, going out even in the worst conditions.[7]

It became increasingly clear that Rev. Moon's training
program and style of unification was decidedly experiential.
Under his direction, the attainment of solidarity within the ranks
would come not as a result of organizational hierarchies,
executive committees, drawn-out stratagems, political
coalitioning, or even a uniform lecture presentation of the
Principle. It would come rather as a result of shared experience.
In January, 1972, that meant hitting the streets of New York
City in mid-winter to sell revival tickets at $6.00 each ($18.00
for three nights) to hear an unknown evangelist. That training
was emphasized as much as visible results was evident both in
that pioneers were not allowed to sell in pairs and in the rule that
tickets be sold only for all three nights. One pioneer well
expressed the existential burden borne by the ticket sellers:

> New York City! Your streets are filled with emptiness.
> How much of our blood is going to be claimed by
> Satan? Were we really equal to the task? Then we
> began to try. And it didn't work. And we would pray
> for strength and courage . . . Then we would be faced
> with ourselves again. Sell a ticket . . . We had to sell
> a ticket . . . We had to go out on the streets by
> ourselves . . . we couldn't go in pairs. People were in
> a hurry or would stop and tell us it was great, but they
> never come in the city at night. Or that we were good
> salesmen but they had another commitment. And
> *nothing* worked. Weren't we giving everything?
> Something deep inside reminded us that there was
> something we were holding back, something that we
> were yet embarrassed about or afraid to do. Then we
> did this thing—honestly, totally—it still didn't work.
> We couldn't even pray then. It was as if we were

entirely deserted . . . We were struggling our absolute
best and losing before we had even started. It was
agony . . . hell. We weren't "we" any longer, but lost
and rejected individuals, each person in his private
desperation.[8]

While pioneers hit the streets, local center members in each
of the seven cities set up speaking dates, rented halls, did
mailings, printed programs, bought ads, "schlepped" posters and
sold tickets wherever possible. In this sense, the tour required
movement-wide coordination as well as increased individual
commitment.

Each revival stop featured opening remarks by local
directors, music by the "Unification Chorale," introductions by
W. Farley Jones (President, Unification Church, U.S.A.) and
three nights of talks by Rev. Moon. Translated from the Korean
first by Young Whi Kim and later in the tour by Bo Hi Pak,
Rev. Moon's topics were "One God, One World Religion,"
"Ideal World for God and Man," and "The New Messiah, and
the Formula of God in History."

Despite the efforts of pioneers and existing centers, the tour
was a constant battle against anonymity and, in the Eastern
cities, against the elements. In New York City bitter weather
limited attendance to between 350-450 people for the three nights
even though many more tickets had been sold.[9] In Washington,
a blizzard not only hindered the turnout but stranded pioneers in
Frederick, Maryland, when the bus carrying them to California
broke down in heavy snow.

On the West Coast, the weather was not a problem. Still, it
was not until Berkeley that the tour had its first full house.
Farley Jones noted:

Through the sixth city it was a struggle. Attendance
was not as great as we had hoped . . . but in Berkeley
. . . there were not enough seats; the program had to

be postponed because the people were still pouring in. Each night was a full house.[10]

There were a number of reasons for the Berkeley success. Perhaps most important, it was the last stop on the tour, and the center there had the longest amount of time to prepare. Following Rev. Moon's early January, 1972, visit to the Bay Area, the Berkeley Center rented a large room (capacity: 700) at the Claremont Hotel and mobilized five committees—Tickets, Literature, Publicity, Physical Arrangements, and Follow-up, to prepare for the March 9-11, 1972, revival.

Apart from the center's initiatives, Berkeley traditionally was fertile ground for new movements of various types, and prior to the tour's arrival, neutral to positive articles appeared in both the *Berkeley Gazette* and *Oakland Tribune*.[11] In addition, the tour had become more polished, and ticket prices were reduced to $6.00 for the three nights. Finally, Rev. Moon, who had suffered with the flu during the first six cities, was in good health for Berkeley. For these reasons, the pioneers finished the seven-city tour with a "feeling of having triumphed."[12]

Although the Berkeley stopover was gratifying, that particular success was less an end than a beginning of the movement's active evangelizing. Far more ambitious crusades were to follow. At the same time, the first priority of the movement continued to be the attainment of *internal solidarity*. This was especially clear at a meeting of Bay Area members and pioneers in San Francisco following the Berkeley revival. In response to a question on how the San Francisco group and the Berkeley group would relate in the future, one pioneer recounted Rev. Moon's "hurricane-like fury at Satan and the division of the American family":

> "They are one!" he thundered. "There is no Miss Kim's group and Mr. Kim's group and Mr. Choi's group. There are no groups. They are all Mr. Moon's group. Missionaries will be recalled to Korea. Members will

be interchanged, and all members will go through my training, even your president Farley Jones."[13]

What Rev. Moon's training called for was a three-year period (1972-74) of total mobilization. The first step in this training involved the selection and assignment of "state representatives" (SRs), "itinerary workers" (IWs), and evangelical bus team members. To coordinate these groups, an entirely new organization was born.

One World Crusade

One World Crusade, Inc. (OWC) was the engine of the Unification Church's evangelistic activities from 1972 through 1974. Through this structure, pioneer state representatives, bus team members and leaders, itinerary workers and existing church centers coordinated activities. The organization, itself, was formed during the Day of Hope revival in Los Angeles, the fifth city of the seven-city tour. An entry from David Kim's missionary diary, dated February 28, 1972, recounts its origins:

> Our Master, in the morning, had a session with five key Family members at Courtney House, the Los Angeles church Center, to discuss the official name of mobile units composed of the 72 first trainees in New York. He said that a new organization should be formed to evangelize the United States and, further, the whole world. The new organization should be incorporated as a non-profit, legal recipient of funds and be self supportive and financially independent. Our Master will be the chairman of the Board of Directors.
> Two probable names were suggested—"World Unification Crusade" and "One World Crusade." After heated discussion, finally "One World Crusade" was born by our Master's decision.[14]

Although the OWC structure included state representatives, itinerary workers, and existing centers, it was especially identified with "mobile unit" bus teams. Originally, The Plan called for single evangelical bus teams on the East and West coasts. Later it was decided that buses would reinforce activities in all fifty states, holding revival meetings and lecturing the Principle message. The goal was for "fifty buses in fifty states carrying 2000 members."[15]

After the conclusion of the seven-city tour in March, 1972, newly appointed OWC "commanders" Young Oon Kim and David Kim, along with approximately twenty-five members each, set out from the Bay Area on separate northern and southern bus team routes to meet in Washington, D.C. the following August. At that time, a third bus team was formed and in December, 1972, seven more teams were organized, making a total of ten evangelical bus teams, each assigned to a specific region of the country. By July 1, 1973, forty more OWC mobile units were organized so that there was a unit for every state. On that foundation, the movement launched more ambitious speaking tours in late 1973 and 1974.

The genius of the OWC was the way in which it integrated a variety of different functions. First and foremost, the OWC fostered evangelistic outreach. At each of their stops, evangelizing bus teams reinforced activities of newly sent out and often solitary state representatives. Witnessing actively, especially on college campuses, bus team members brought guests to evening programs, conducted workshops and left long lists of contacts for local state representatives to follow up. Seven day crusades in each state frequently resulted in the recruitment of permanent members.

Equally important, the OWC enhanced the movement's internal solidarity. The mobile units combined membership from various parts of the movement and continued the process of unification begun at the original pioneer training session. At the same time, the establishment of state representatives and itinerary workers as well as such publications as *Pioneer's Progress* (which supplanted Miss Kim's *New Age Frontiers* from July to October, 1972) opened channels of movement-wide communication. The OWC effectively linked up disparate centers throughout the country.

In addition to evangelistic outreach and organizational integration, the OWC helped lay the groundwork for the movement's future speaking tours. Members cultivated important contacts and gained public relations experience. Actively contacting news media, local churches, and civic officials, public relations teams stressed theistic principles and ethical values. These themes were reflected in "Rallies for God" on college campuses and at state capitol buildings.

This campaigning was confrontational in the early 1970s as rallies for God, and as often for America, paired off against anti-Vietnam War demonstrations. In Austin, Texas, twenty-seven "heavenly troops" challenged 360 radicals at the State Capitol building.[16] Martial imagery and discipline, however, was valuable training for the movement's later speaking tours. So, too, was the crusade's mobility. From March 16, 1972, when the two evangelical bus teams left San Francisco, until August 1, 1972, when they arrived in Washington, D.C., Mobile Unit #1 (the northern bus) campaigned in twenty-two cities and twenty-two states, traveling a total of 8,400 miles. Mobile Unit #2 (the southern bus) campaigned in twenty-one cities and twenty states, traveling a total of 7,780 miles.[17]

The ecumenical thrust, political campaigning, martial discipline, and mobility of the OWC not only helped prepare the movement for future campaigns but also signaled the rise of David S.C. Kim. Of the three missionary groups, "United Faith, Inc." had most emphasized the ecumenical dimension stressed in the crusade. His own political background was helpful in the crusade's public relations work. Similarly, the martial discipline and confrontational aspects of the crusade were consistent with his self-image as "a fighter."[18] Finally, the long distances he was forced to travel as missionary to the Northwest had prepared him for the mobility of evangelical team buses.

For these reasons, it was Mr. Kim rather than Miss Kim who emerged as the OWC's leading "field general." In over forty separate reports under such titles as "Marching Across This Great Land to Make It Free," "One World Crusade Is Marching On," and "Mobile Unit II Moves West Coast States," David Kim chronicled bus team activities in 1972.[19] In December of that year, he was named "Executive Director" of the One World Crusade.

Although the evangelical bus teams originally set out from the San Francisco Bay Area in mid-March, 1972, it was not until mid-October that any of the OWC mobile units returned. A homecoming for David Kim's Mobile Unit II featured an October 17th 'Rally for God' on Sproul Plaza at the University of California at Berkeley, interviews with the *Berkeley Gazette* and *Oakland Tribune*, and complete lecture presentations to seven new contacts.

Proceeding across the Bay to Mr. Choi's International Pioneer Academy, bus team members held a "Rally for God" at Civic Center Park across from the San Francisco Public Library on October 20, 1972. While over one hundred San Francisco members handed out pamphlets, One World Crusade staged what David Kim called "one of our most enthusiastic rallies."[20]

Having arrived in the Bay Area from Portland and Eugene, Oregon where crusades were held from October 7-14, Mr. Kim's bus team continued on to Las Vegas, Nevada; Tempe, Arizona; Albuquerque, New Mexico; and Austin, Texas, by December, 1972. With other bus teams equally mobile, the movement was under considerable pressure to fuel the crusade. To help do so, another new organization was born.

Mobile Fundraising Teams

If the One World Crusade was the foundation of the movement's evangelistic activities from 1972-74, door-to-door and street-corner solicitation, or "fundraising" (generally with candles) was its means of economic support. Because of the urgent need for existing centers to help support OWC mobile units and pioneer centers in the field, as well as their own activities, aggressive fundraising campaigns came to be favored over either businesses or outside employment.

Existing centers, pioneers, and OWC evangelical bus units all undertook fundraising campaigns, but they became especially identified with a new institution, the mobile fundraising team (MFT). Consisting of eight or nine full-time sellers, MFTs first formed in late August, 1972. The original two teams on each coast merged into one permanent team of fourteen members in October, 1972, and expanded to three teams and thirty-six sellers by the following September. In October, 1973, a fourth team was added and by the following May, there were eight teams and eighty members.[21] Their selling efforts not only supported evangelistic activities of the OWC but also helped the movement to purchase properties and conduct its later speaking tours.

As organizational developments, there were several important parallels between the OWC and MFT. Both were aggressive and mobile. Both consolidated otherwise scattered local efforts. And both were born of necessity in response to the demands of a specific campaign. For the OWC, this was the seven-city tour. For the MFT, it was the "Belvedere Project," a movement-wide, late summer and early autumn 1972 campaign to raise the funds necessary to purchase Belvedere, a Tarrytown, New York estate as the movement's international training center. To understand the origins of MFTs and their impact it is necessary to highlight, in somewhat greater detail, the movement's fundraising efforts both prior to and following the Belvedere Project. A three-stage development is clearly evident: those activities predating the campaign, the campaign itself, and the establishment of permanent MFTs following the campaign.

Economic support had been a continuous and frequently divisive problem for the movement prior to the Belvedere Project. Outside employment hindered full-time evangelism, and businesses were no less time consuming and often distracting. As early as 1961, Miss Kim's Bay Area group experimented with door-to-door sales as a means of economic support and witnessing. In 1967, the Washington Center tried to do the same with "Holiday Magic" cosmetics. That same center was more successful selling wholesale notions in a 1970 Christmas drive for new songbooks. Still, with other centers dabbling in a variety of economic ventures, members were forced to admit during the 1971 reconsolidation conference that they "have yet to come up with something that all the centers can do."[22]

Following Rev. Moon's arrival and seven-city tour, the need for funds became acute. Farley Jones spoke of "facing great financial struggles in the coming months and years."[23] Ironically, one breakthrough came as a result of the breakdown of the seven-city tour's missionary bus in Frederick, Maryland, when members found that they could garner donations. This realization, combined with the increased financial demands of national mobilization, led to more sustained fundraising efforts. In April, 1972, the Washington, D.C., center surpassed a goal of $4,000 profit through door-to-door sales of candles produced in the basement of the College Park, Maryland, center. Also supplied with College Park candles, the New York Center netted $1,600 in nine days toward a three-month goal of $21,000. In Philadelphia, the center set aside one night a week for regular candle selling.

Candle selling proliferated rapidly among the existing centers. They had, finally, "come up with something that all the centers could do." Still, there was a lack of coordination. In his OWC reports, David Kim spoke of financial burdens and the lack of funds from headquarters. As a consequence, OWC mobile units and pioneer centers began fundraising for expenses. Thus, although fundraising became the movement's predominant economic means, there was no center or focus.

Rev. Moon solved the problem of coordinating fundraising activity in 1972, when he directed the American movement "to find a large property in New York suitable for use as . . . (an) international training center."[24] The assignment was given to New York center director Philip Burley, who found Belvedere three days after it had been put on the market. Situated on the Hudson River thirty miles north of New York City in Tarrytown, the twenty-two acre, $850,000 estate was described in a brochure sent to Rev. Moon in Korea, and he said to buy it. At that point, Miss Kim left her bus team to negotiate for the property. Succeeding both in committing the seller to her and in extending the stipulated thirty days payment allowance to ninety days, she faced the major problem of raising a $294,000 down payment.

From mid-July through mid-August, 1972, Miss Kim traveled throughout the country securing personal loans. By late August, her efforts needed to be supplemented by efforts of the American movement. Because the Maryland center had had success selling its own manufactured candles, it was decided to try that "as a national effort to raise money for the large down payment."[25] With forty-seven days to go until the payment was due, the Belvedere Project was launched in earnest.

While obtaining the necessary funds was primary, the project was also significant in that it promoted solidarity. Miss Kim noted, "For seven weeks nearly every member in our Family, in every state, abandoned all other activities to sell candles." There was total mobilization. State representatives, pioneer centers, OWC teams, and existing centers all pledged themselves to specific goals in order to meet the overall goal of $36,000 profit per week. *Pioneer's Progress*, initially instituted as an evangelistic bulletin, became instead a report of the latest developments on Belvedere.

The feeling was exhilaration. One project coordinator exclaimed, "Never has there been a project like this in the whole American movement!" Farley Jones enthused "This is the greatest thing we've ever done because it is our first national project for a unitary goal." Similar sentiments were voiced by a candle-seller who asserted, "When it's over, we'll know that every American has paid for Belvedere. . . and we'll know that we've paid for it with everything we've got."[26]

Aside from promoting internal solidarity, the Belvedere Project prompted several innovations. One of these was the development of candle "factories." With Anchor Hocking six-ounce Brandy Snifters and Amoco paraffin "piled floor to ceiling," the College Park, Maryland factory relocated to the six room basement of a recently purchased farm in Upper Marlboro. By the second week of the project, production had gone "from eight hundred to twelve hundred dozen a week," and was expected to reach "peak production of 1,700 dozen a week, or about 250 dozen (3,000 candles) a day."[27] A similar factory with a rotating crew was set up in the Denver center garage, and a third factory was operated by the Berkeley Center out of a warehouse in Concord, twenty miles away.

"Still-warm" candles were delivered by another Belvedere innovation, "express candle vans." In the East, vans were dispatched to Chicago, New York, and Atlanta among other cities. The most important innovation of the Belvedere Project, however, was the formation, for the first time, of mobile fundraising teams. As reported in *Pioneers' Progress*,

> Since the end of August, 29 members from across
> the nation have been traveling on two mobile teams —
> one on each coast—and selling candles full time.[28]

The sixteen-member West Coast team included two members from Los Angeles, three from Denver, two from Kansas City, and nine from the Berkeley Center.

As a result of total mobilization and these innovations, the Belvedere Project ended in victory. Miss Kim wrote, "By the deadline, through loans I had secured, through efforts of our international Family, but primarily through candle sales in America, we made the down payment."[29] At 1:00 p.m., October 10, 1972, the caretaker of Belvedere received a call from the seller saying that, from that moment, "Belvedere is in new hands." Later that day, members arrived to explore the house and grounds. The feeling was best summarized in Miss Kim's questions to the 'new owners':

> How can you describe a miracle? ... Now you have
> seen Belvedere. Is it better than your dreams?[30]

Given the results of the Belvedere Project, the movement
took steps to institute fundraising on a permanent basis.
Belvedere Project Assistant Keith Cooperrider noted, "We found
that people, cut off from normal center activities and given the
sole responsibility of selling, could do phenomenally well."
Thus, on October 19, 1972, after a week of "rest and
recuperation," fourteen members of the newly formed permanent
MFT arrived in Philadelphia to begin four months of candle
selling. This team, composed largely of members of the former
Belvedere Project mobile teams (including five from the Berkeley
Center), was to sell candles for eight hours a day, five days a
week, to achieve its goal of earning $18,500 each month.[31]

Although monetary goals were important, the MFT "spirit"
also took hold. As one member noted, "Every conversation was
laced with candle-selling stories, for everyone had a special
experience." It was this dynamic between material needs and the
meaning fundraising had for members—not the movement's
material needs alone—that led to MFT expansion. Farley Jones
summarized the development well in his "send-off" speech to the
new MFT members:

> At this moment, we are building a new structure in the
> dispensation. . . . I know it will evolve and become a
> greater part of our movement. In a new way you are
> pioneering.[32]

First ICUS Conference

If the MFT was a pioneer effort in finances, the first
International Conference on Unified Science (later renamed the
International Conference on the Unity of the Sciences, or ICUS),
was a parallel undertaking in education and the sciences. Held
November 23-26, 1972, at the Waldorf-Astoria Hotel in New

York City, the conference brought together twenty scientists from seven nations to discuss "Moral Orientation of the Sciences."

The previous January, Rev. Moon, in the midst of preparations for the seven-city tour suggested the idea to Edward Haskell, a lecturer at Southern Connecticut State College and chairman of the Council for Unified Research and Education (CURE).[33] Haskell, who had been contacted by the New Haven center in the fall of 1970, was enthusiastic about the proposal and helped draw up plans for the coming autumn.

As with the One World Crusade and mobile fundraising teams, the Unified Science Conference fulfilled several objectives at once. First, it was intended to be a contribution to society. In his closing address, "The Role of Unified Science in the Moral Orientation of the World," Rev. Moon emphasized human happiness, cultural advancement, the "reformation of spiritual life . . . by establishing a new standard of value," the unity of science and religion, and the establishment on earth of the ideal unified world.[34] In pursuit of these ends, conference organizers gathered scientists from private industry, Yale, Harvard, Columbia, and Oxford.

The conference further enhanced the movement's internal solidarity by integrating diverse educational and cultural activities, be they Koinonia projects, student groups, or the events of Mr. Choi's Re-Education Foundation. At the same time, the conference showcased the movement and its versatility. As noted in *New Age Frontiers*, "The whole conference staff—administrators, typists, hostesses, messengers, security guards, PR men, and photographers—were family members."[35] No less than OWC or MFT, ICUS further developed movement sophistication.

The conference itself included an opening banquet and three working days of lectures, responses, panels and open discussions on a number of themes, such as "Tools for Solution of Scientific Problems: Metatheory," chaired by Dr. Nicholas Kurti of Oxford University and Fellow of the Royal Society; "Application of

Unisci Tools: Solutions of Key Problems," chaired by Dr. William V. Quine of Harvard University; and "Concrete Applications of Unified Science Solutions," chaired by Dr. Ervin Laszo of the Genesco College of the State University of New York.

The conference was successful both in the quality of presentations and as a building block for future conferences. The movement published the proceedings in a volume entitled *Moral Orientation of the Sciences* and held the Second International Conference on Unified Science the following November in Tokyo. Expanded guest lists and formats would characterize the annual ICUS.

Meeting the Politicos

Meeting political leaders was equally important. The movement was, in Rev. Moon's words, "preparing on two fronts." As he described them, "one was to work to unify Christianity, i.e. the evangelical movement, the Divine Principle movement. The other was "to prepare for the fight against Communism, i.e., the Anti-Communist movement."[36] In America, the Freedom Leadership Foundation (FLF) spearheaded the movement's Victory Over Communism (VOC) effort since 1969. It was through this organization that Rev. Moon met a number of United States senators and congressmen in the early months of 1973.

As with its previous organizational initiatives, these meetings accomplished several purposes simultaneously. First and foremost, they were a chance to clearly outline the movement's opposition to Marxism. One member present during these meetings noted, "Rev. Moon discussed national and international problems, stressing the danger of communism. He often mentioned that the United States was still the communists' main target.

While these concerns were primary, the meetings also enhanced the movement's twin organizational objectives of internal solidarity and versatility. Rev. Moon, in meeting with Congressional leaders, legitimated the movement's political involvement, still a sore point for some members. Furthermore, as members were responsible for public relations arrangements, coverage, and follow up, the meetings once again enhanced the movement's versatility and sophistication.

The meetings, themselves, culminated FLF's activities in Washington, D.C. Having made numerous contacts through public demonstrations, forums and, most importantly, through bi-weekly publication of *The Rising Tide*, billed as "America's Fastest Growing Freedom Newspaper", FLF arranged for Rev. Moon in February, 1973, to meet Admiral Bender, Commandant of the U.S. Coast Guard, Senators Edward Kennedy of Massachusetts, Jesse Helms (R), North Carolina; Hubert Humphrey (D), Minnesota; Strom Thurmond (R), South Carolina; William Brock (R) Tennessee; and James Buckley (Conservative), New York; and representatives Richard Ichord (D), Missouri; William Mailliard (R) California; Earl Landgrebe (R) Indiana; Guy Vander Jagt (R) California; Floyd Spencer (R) South Carolina; Philip Crane (R) Illinois; and Trent Lott, (R) Mississippi. On April 5, 1973, Rev. Moon met with visiting President of South Vietnam, Nguyen Van Thieu. According to FLF Special Assistant, Mike Leone, "The meetings were very, very successful. . . . All ran over their allotted half hour, many lasted for an hour."[37]

A National Movement Emerges

By July 1, 1973, midway through its three year period (1972-74) of "total mobilization," the Unification Church was emerging as a national movement. It had attained organizational solidarity through the One World Crusade which as of July, 1973, had mobile units in all fifty states, and its versatility had been demonstrated through initiatives in evangelization, finances, the sciences, and politics. Still, the Unification Church was largely invisible to the public. The seven-city tour attracted only marginal notice in the press. Mobile Fundraising Teams, although growing, attracted virtually no notice. The Science Conference was reviewed only in isolated scientific journals, and Rev. Moon's meetings with Congressmen were private.

However, during the second eighteen months of its revival period, the Unification Church attracted nationwide coverage. Four internal developments were foundational in this development. The first of these was the expansion of the OWC and a re-shuffling of local leadership. Although center members had been called to pioneer missions as state representatives or as OWC mobile unit members, the leadership of existing centers had remained intact. However in December 1972, center directors were assigned as new bus team leaders."[38] Included among the new bus team leaders were Farley Jones, President of HSA-UWC, America, and Edwin Ang, director of the Berkeley center, who became a bus team leader in New England.

With the dispersion of local directors, leadership in the existing centers was re-shuffled. Neil Salonen was named acting director of the Washington, D.C., center and acting president of HSA-UWC while Farley Jones was in the field. Two members from Edwin Ang's Berkeley Center were named directors of centers in Philadelphia and St. Louis. David Hose, from Mr. Choi's Re-Education Foundation, moved across the Bay to take charge of the Berkeley center. Joe Tully, also from the Re-Education Foundation, was called to New York City to assume responsibilities there. The effect of these changes was to maximize the movement's national thrust while avoiding local distractions.

Equally important as the expansion of OWC mobile units and the re-shuffling of center directors was the arrival of 109 European members on January 15, 1973. This "new pilgrim movement", as Rev. Moon termed it, was the result of pledges extracted from European church leaders. After a two-week

there was a nation-wide network of support. David Kim summarized Rev. Moon's role in the overall development:

> By July 1, 1973, only 18 months after His arrival in the U.S., He had brought phenomenal results. He had completed already one seven-city public speaking tour in major cities on both coasts of the U.S. He had raised the infant Unification Church to nationwide cooperation through the One World Crusade. He had strengthened and enlarged each group to serve all 50 states. Further, He had set up an International Leadership Training Program at the Belvedere Estate. During this same period of time, He initiated and spoke at the First International Conference on Unified Science to begin His efforts to develop a God-centered science and technology which can truly satisfy every man's desire for material happiness.[43]

Symbolic of the "turning point" the movement had reached half-way through its three-year revival period was the proclamation of July 1, 1973, as the "Day of Resolution for Victory." In effect, the task of attaining internal solidarity was finished. What followed during the second eighteen-month period of evangelism was an all-out campaign by the movement to attain public visibility.

Day of Hope and Celebration of Life Tours

While the drive for increased membership continued unabated from 1972-74, the emphasis of the movement for the eighteen months following its July 1, 1973 Resolution for Victory was on intensely publicized public speaking tours. During this period, the movement conducted four separate tours: a twenty-one city Day of Hope tour, a thirty-two city Day of Hope tour, a ten-city "Celebration of Life" tour and a culminating eight-city Day of Hope tour.

These tours were much larger than the original seven-city tour of 1972 and far more sophisticated. More important, the motivation behind the tours was not the building of internal solidarity but the attainment of public visibility. Following completion of the twenty-one city and thirty-two city tours, Rev. Moon had spoken publicly in all fifty states. Well before the Celebration of Life and the culminating eight-city tour, the movement had attained national exposure.

Twenty-One City tour. The twenty-one city tour, which began on October 1, 1973, was both similar and different from the earlier seven-city tour. Like the previous tour, the this one included three nights of talks by Rev. Moon. However, unlike the previous one, the twenty-one city tour was more provocative. Taking as its theme, "Christianity in Crisis: New Hope," each three-night stop featured speeches by Rev. Moon on "God's Hope for Man," "God's Hope for America," and "The Future of Christianity."

Although the twenty-one city tour was far more ambitious than the earlier seven-city tour, the movement had more time to mobilize. In mid-July, as a result of a further influx of missionaries from Japan and Europe, two forty-member IOWC teams were formed to travel the twenty-one city itinerary, preparing the way for Rev. Moon's lecture series the following fall and winter. By the end of August, more than four hundred members gathered to publicize the Day of Hope talks scheduled to begin at Carnegie Hall on October 1st.

Besides mobilizing members, the movement sought to generate media coverage. For this purpose it organized a five-member Day of Hope planning staff. Consisting of a campaign coordinator, PR director, media director, technical director, and logistics coordinator, the accent was on public visibility. Newspaper and magazine ads, bus and commuter train posters, and mass leafletting introduced the series to the people of each city. The staff sent professionally made tapes to 540 radio stations for public service announcements. According to campaign coordinator Mike Leone, the purpose of the staff's work was two-fold: first, "to bring to the public eye Rev. Moon of South Korea, a dynamic and inspiring spiritual leader of thousands of people," and second, "to fill every hall, every night."[44]

In addition to personnel mobilization and saturation advertising, two other innovations of the twenty-one city tour greatly enhanced the movement's public visibility. The obtaining of civic proclamations was the first of these. The previous February 14, 1973, as a result of the intercessory efforts of Benjamin Swig, a prominent San Francisco hotel owner and friend of Mr. Choi, Rev. Moon was awarded the key to the city of San Francisco.[45] During the twenty-one city tour, campaign workers secured a multitude of proclamations of honorary citizenship, and days, or weeks, of "Hope and Unification."[46]

Many of these proclamations were read at a second major innovation of the tour, "Day of Hope" banquets. Held prior to opening night talks during the tour, the kick-off dinners featured entertainment, introductions and greetings from Rev. Moon. With guest lists including civic and religious leaders, educators and businessmen, these were another important means of attaining public visibility.

The results of the twenty-one city tour were remarkable. In New York, where four hundred members worked a month prior to the Carnegie Hall opening, the movement attracted widespread media coverage. The September 22, 1973, New York *Daily News* carried a large photo and article on a Day of Hope rally on the steps of Federal Hall on Wall Street. *Time, Newsweek* and *Christianity Today* all carried somewhat quizzical stories on the campaign. Associated Press religion writer George W. Cornell's generally positive feature story on the Day of Hope and the Unification Church appeared in seventy-nine newspapers throughout the U.S. However, whether skeptical or positive, the movement was achieving the goal of public visibility.

Two hundred and fifty prominent New Yorkers attended the inaugural "Day of Hope" banquet at the Waldorf Astoria Hotel. Telegrams of congratulations were read from New York mayor,

John V. Lindsay and columnist William F. Buckley, Jr., as well as from several U.S. congressmen. In Baltimore, Cardinal Sheehan sent his blessing to the banquet. In Washington, D.C., where the movement again concentrated its efforts, almost four hundred citizens turned out for the banquet, and more than three thousand people for the three nights of talks at Lisner Auditorium. In Atlanta, Georgia Governor Jimmy Carter, proclaimed November 7, 1973, a "Day of Hope and Unification." Though similar proclamations were issued throughout the midwest, the movement concentrated efforts in the media and policy making centers of New York and Washington, D.C.

The twenty-one city tour came to the Bay Area in January, 1974. With months to plan and a substantial number of local contacts, the January 17, 1974, San Francisco Day of Hope banquet attracted more than 500 guests to Benjamin Swig's Fairmont Hotel. In Berkeley, where Rev. Moon spoke at Zellerbach Auditorium on the University of California campus, *The Daily Californian* reported, "Rev. Moon's followers have waged one of the neatest and best-run publicity campaigns seen here in years."[47] In San Jose, January 17-24, 1974, was proclaimed "Hope and Unification Week" while, in Oakland, Mayor John H. Reading proclaimed the period from January 21-24, 1974, as "Day of Hope Days." Single days of "Hope and Unification" were proclaimed in Berkeley and Hayward, and on January 21, 1974, Rev. Moon was awarded the key to the city of Berkeley by Mayor Warren Widener.

Thirty-two city tour. Following the completion of the twenty-one city tour in Los Angeles on January 29, 1974, the movement immediately launched another Day of Hope tour with the theme "The New Future of Christianity." This tour, which carried the Day of Hope to thirty-two American cities in sixty-four days, included an opening night banquet and a second night speech by Rev. Moon at each stop.

With the completion of the thirty-two city tour, Rev. Moon had proclaimed his message publicly in all fifty states. To conduct campaigns in this drive from Maine to Hawaii, three IOWC advance teams from the twenty-one city tour were increased to seven teams of seventy members. Each of these teams were given itineraries for four or five two-week campaigns in preparation for the Day of Hope programs. According to Rev. Moon, the tour had "created in two weeks a foundation in every state which would have taken two or three years otherwise."[48]

Celebration of Life. The movement hoped to reap a harvest of new members as a result of the Day of Hope tours. To facilitate these goals, the Sun Myung Moon Christian Crusade (SMCC) sponsored a ten-city "Celebration of Life" tour that evangelized a selected city in each of the ten regions of the country. Beginning in the Bay Area, the itinerary included stops in Seattle, St Paul, Minnesota; Austin, Texas; New Orleans; Miami, Florida; Columbus, Ohio; Louisville, Kentucky; Boston; and Rochester, New York.

Billed as "A 21st Century Experience," programs included an hour and fifteen minutes of entertainment: songs, solos, skits, dances, and testimonials, followed by forty-five minutes of inspiration from "God's Colonel" Bo Hi Pak, on key points of the Unification Principle. Week-long stops in each city featured Wednesday, Thursday, and Friday performances and a weekend Celebration of Life workshop. Rather than preaching crisis, the concern was to find a successful formula of mass evangelization.

As a result of tour innovations, advance preparation, and media coverage, the Celebration of Life drew substantial crowds. SMCC's "World Premiere" May 15-17, 1974, at the Paramount Theatre in Oakland drew 2,600 guests and thirty-four participants for a weekend workshop in the Santa Cruz Mountains. By Boston, the three-day total was up to 7,562.[49] Equally important was the emergence of New Hope Singers International and the Korean Folk Ballet. Both would make signal contributions to the movement's culminating eight-city tour, scheduled to begin in September, 1974 at Madison Square Garden.

Finances

Although the financial burden of conducting its Day of Hope speaking tours was considerable, the movement found that tour costs could be turned to advantage. Large expenditures were, in themselves, a means of attaining public visibility. Thus movement spokespersons were not hesitant to release budget allotments for the twenty-one city tour ($400,000), thirty-two city tour ($200,000) and the coming eight-city tour ($1,000,000).[50]

The same dynamic was at work in the movement's real estate acquisitions. In addition to Belvedere, the nearby Exquisite Acres (renamed East Garden) was purchased on October 10, 1973, for $625,000. The former St. Joseph's Seminary, located on 250 acres, some sixty miles to the north in Barrytown, New York, was purchased on January 21, 1974, at a cost of $1.5 million. Also, by 1974, the movement had purchased nearly 300 acres of greenbelt land in Tarrytown, New York, putting the total value of its Hudson Valley acquisitions at approximately $3 million.

Sources of church income generated additional publicity. American HSA-UWC President Neil Salonen estimated 1974 church income in the United States to be $8 million, up from $100,000 in 1971. Contributions, according to Salonen, came almost entirely from street sales of peanuts, candles, flowers, and dry-flower arrangements. Fundraising, though undertaken in all centers, was spearheaded by the expanding mobile fundraising teams, which by the spring of 1974 split into a "National Headquarters' MFT" for general church expenses and "Father's MFT" for special projects. Additional monies came in from overseas. More important than American resources was fundraising in Japan. There, since 1972, the Japanese family fielded 120 seven-day-a-week flower-selling teams. Funding from Japan, however, was not public knowledge.

What was public knowledge was the church's industrial holdings in Korea. There, in the late 1960s and early 1970s, the church initiated a number of economic ventures. Again, these holdings, no less than tour expenditures, were, in themselves, a means of attaining public visibility. That they were freely acknowledged was evident in that Rev. Moon's calling card listed him as chairman of the board of five companies: Tongil Industrial Company, Ltd., a manufacturer of machine parts; Il Hwa Pharmaceutical Company, which produced ginseng tea; the Ilshin Handicraft Company which produced stone vases (marketed in Japan); and two titanium companies, producers of paints and coating materials.[51]

Cultural Affiliates

If the movement's evangelistic crusades and finances generated a degree of public visibility, the same was also true of its cultural affiliates.

The International Cultural Foundation (ICF) founded in Japan by Rev. Moon in 1968, moved its headquarters to 18 East 71st Street, New York City, in December, 1973. Incorporated there as "a non-profit organization dedicated to promoting academic, scientific and cultural exchange among the countries of the world,"[52] it assumed sponsorship of the International Conference on the Unity of Sciences.

A second educational and cultural affiliate, the Korean Cultural and Freedom Foundation (KCFF) was organized in Washington, D.C., by Bo Hi Pak in 1964. The foundation promoted the Children's Relief Fund, Radio of Free Asia, and, most notably, the Little Angels. Conceived of as a Korean answer to the Vienna Boys' Choir, the Little Angels conducted their first KCFF sponsored world tour from September 27 through December 16, 1965. A performance in Gettysburg, Pennsylvania, at the home of former President Dwight Eisenhower (a KCFF board member), an appearance on the nationally-televised Ed Sullivan Show, and seventy-five performances throughout the United States highlighted the inaugural tour. By 1974, the Little Angels had completed seven world tours, traveled over 200,000 miles, and given 1,100 performances, including command performances at the White House and London Palladium.[53]

Although performances were kept free of church advocacy, one exception was the Little Angels' Holiday Benefit Performance for UNICEF at the U.N. General Assembly Hall. Rev. Moon was listed in a brochure as Founder and honored at the performance with a standing ovation. Earlier that fall, the church had sponsored three benefit performances of the Little Angels in Tarrytown, New York.

The Collegiate Association for the Research of Principles (CARP), founded by church members at Waseda University, Japan, in 1964. began in the United States in November, 1973. Once organized, it ran annual International Leadership Seminars (ILS). The first of these brought eighty-seven graduate students from Tokyo University, Japan, and 120 students from several universities in England. The second, held July 15 through August 23, 1974, at the Unification Church's International Training Center in Barrytown, New York, attracted 219 students from England, France, Germany, Japan and from Korean residents in Japan.[54]

Watergate

A key factor which attracting national attention to the emergent movement was its involvement in the Watergate crisis. Previously, the movement had separated evangelistic and religious-political activities through the separate incorporation of the Freedom Leadership Foundation. This separation broke down during the Watergate crisis. In asserting that "the crisis for America is a crisis for God," the movement's well-orchestrated demonstrations in support of President Richard Nixon, more than any other single factor, catapulted it into the national spotlight. It also alienated the church from significant sections of the populace.[55]

The movement launched a forty-day National Prayer and Fast for the Watergate Crisis (NPFWC) on December 1, 1973.

This action took place following a two week break in the twenty-one city "Day of Hope" tour during which time Rev. Moon traveled to Japan and Korea. The decision to launch the campaign was finalized in Omaha, Nebraska, and conducted simultaneously with the remainder of the twenty-one city tour.

Asserting, "God's command at this crossroads in American History is to Forgive, Love, and Unite," Rev. Moon's "Answer to Watergate" statement appeared in full page advertisements purchased in newspapers in each of the twenty-one cities of the Day of Hope itinerary, including the *New York Times* and the *Washington Post*, beginning November 30, 1973. Over the next two months, it was published in one newspaper in every state except Hawaii. In addition, The National Prayer and Fast for the Watergate Crisis Committee (NPFWC) organized vigils, rallies, letter-writing, and leafletting in all fifty states to publicize its theme and to obtain signatures of people promising to pray and fast for the Watergate crisis. At least eight senators and fifty-three congressmen either signed the statement or responded with messages of support.[56] Congressman Guy Vander Jagt (R-Michigan) read Rev. Moon's Watergate statement into the *Congressional Record* of December 21, 1973.

Two annual events on the Washington, D.C., calendar were also occasions for calling national attention to the Unification Church. The first was the December 14, 1973, Christmas Tree Lighting, where the movement mobilized 1,200 pennant-waving, banner-carrying members. Not only was this rally aired on nationwide television, but later in the evening, President Nixon emerged from the White House to thank NPFWC President Neil Salonen and still-assembled members for their support.[57]

The other annual event of note was the January 31, 1974, Presidential Prayer Breakfast to which Rev. Moon was invited. Although plans to ring the Washington Hilton Hotel, site of the prayer breakfast, were canceled, a post-breakfast rally at Lafayette Park brought out Edward and Tricia Nixon Cox, who greeted well-wishers. On February 1, 1974, Rev. Moon had a twenty minute audience with President Nixon, reportedly telling him, "Don't knuckle under to pressure. Stand up for your convictions."[58]

A second phase of the church's Watergate involvement came at the height of the crisis in 1974. With court-ruled limitations on executive privilege, articles of impeachment, and exposure of damaging transcripts of presidential conversations all imminent, the NPFWC mobilized 610 members for a three-day fast and vigil on the steps of the Capitol Building in Washington, D.C., July 22-24, 1974. Participants wore placards with a quotation from Rev. Moon's Watergate statement on the back and a picture of the elected or appointed official for whom they were praying on the front.

With public attention riveted on Watergate, the three-day vigil received national exposure. Seventy-six congressmen and five senators came out to meet the person praying for them. Newspapers across the nation carried pictures and interviews in over 350 stories. Local television stations and all three broadcasting networks showed film of the event and described it in their newscasts. Among the news magazines sending their own reporters to cover the vigil were *Time*, *Newsweek*, *New Republic*, *U.S. News and World Report*, *New Yorker*, and the *Washingtonian*. Rabbi Baruch Korff, organizer of the Citizens' Committee for Fairness to the President, came to the vigil and declared "personal solidarity with these young people."[59] Nationally syndicated columnist Art Buchwald later wrote a column featuring an imaginary conversation between one "Senator Throggsmutton" and the young man fasting for him.[60]

Madison Square Garden

The culmination of the movement's drive for public visibility was its concluding eight-city Day of Hope tour, which opened at New York's Madison Square Garden, September 18, 1974. Building on all that had gone before, the tour was, in certain respects, a triumphant march through many of the same cities in the movement's original, anonymous, seven-city tour of 1972. Taking as its theme, "The New Future of Christianity," the itinerary included New York City, Washington D.C., Atlanta, Chicago, Seattle, San Francisco and Los Angeles. However, the key to the eight-city tour was success at Madison Square Garden.

Although Madison Square Garden was its most ambitious undertaking to date, the movement had several months to prepare. In addition, previous efforts had led to, in American HSA-UWC President Neil Salonen's words, "a tremendous influx of members."[61] In New York City, members of the seven local churches had been assigned, since July, one hundred and twenty houses each for door-to-door contact. Ten thousand pocket sized editions of *Divine Principle* and an equal number of Rev. Moon's "Christianity in Crisis" talks were made ready for distribution.

The arrival of seven hundred IOWC members in mid-August greatly augmented campaign preparations in New York City. Lodged at the Paris Hotel on Manhattan's West Side, ten seventy-member IOWC teams followed rigorous street canvassing schedules in assigned sections of Manhattan and Queens. Representatives from each of the forty nations where the Unification Church maintained missions and the remaining American church members (in all, about two thousand), who converged on New York City for a final week-long blitz prior to September 18th, swelled the ranks still further.

Tickets for the event were free (according to media accounts, over 380,000 had been distributed)[62] and five hundred buses were chartered to transport outlying residents to the Garden. The movement generated further publicity through numerous T.V. and radio "shorts," through full-page ads in the *New York Times*, and through its massive poster campaign. Advertising that "September 18 Could Be Your Re-Birthday," eighty thousand two-by-three-foot posters with a portrait of Rev. Moon as well as insets of the New Hope Singers International and the Korean Folk Ballet "wallpapered" Manhattan. Maintaining 150-200 locations, a twenty-one member postering team put up two thousand posters in forays from midnight until 10:00 a.m., beginning forty days before the rally. As reported in the *New York Times*, "His face is everywhere, it seems."[63]

Given that the movement was able to bring only 350-450 people to Alice Tully Hall in the Lincoln Center for its initial "Day of Hope" tour just thirty-two months earlier the turnout at Madison Square Garden was astounding. The movement feted 1,600 prominent New Yorkers at a kick-off banquet in the Waldorf Astoria on September 17, 1974. The following night, an estimated ten to thirty-five thousand ticket holders were turned away from an already filled-to-capacity Madison Square Garden.[64] With nearly two hundred press people in attendance, widespread publicity helped insure success in other cities.[65] The pattern of overflow crowds and widespread publicity was repeated throughout the tour.[66]

The time bomb is ticking

The Unification Church attained its goal of public visibility by the end of 1974. As in its previous objective of internal solidarity, the movement's genius was the way in which its initiatives were mutually reinforcing. The crowds for its concluding eight-city Day of Hope tour were not only the result of campaign preparations but also the result of interest generated through the movement's diverse involvements. At the same time, these involvements were increasingly questioned. Now that the movement had emerged, it was a visible target. As Rev. Moon put it during an otherwise exuberant celebration at Belvedere following his Madison Square Garden speech, "The time bomb is ticking. We must do our job before the time bomb explodes."[67]

Opposition toward the movement was evident on all fronts but most apparent in controversies over evangelizing. The Bay Area was an early locale of controversy. There, during Rev. Moon's twenty-one city "Day of Hope" tour stop in Berkeley, the Christian Student Coalition of the University of California formally disavowed "any spiritual kinship with the Unification Church and its founder, Sun Myung Moon," purchased a full-page advertisement in the *Daily Californian* to that effect, and distributed leaflets outside Zellerbach Auditorium.[68] Although there had been sporadic protests and picketing previously, this was the first joint effort.

As a result of increased visibility following his meeting with Richard Nixon, Rev. Moon faced mounting opposition during his thirty-two city Day of Hope tour. "Nix-on Moon" placards denounced Rev. Moon as a fascist backed by U.S. money. More common were disruptions during speeches by fundamentalist Christians exhorting audiences and calling Rev. Moon a false prophet. A widely reprinted February 15, 1974, Laurence Stern and William R. MacKaye article in the *Washington Post* quoted the General Secretary of the Korean National Council of Churches, who labeled the movement "a cult . . . a new sect which has been undermining the established church."[69]

Equally significant was a widely circulated document originating in Louisville, Kentucky, entitled, "The Satanic Beliefs of Rev. Moon." Purporting to be from a group of inter-denominational ministers and laymen known as the "Concerned Christians," the return address was the Southern Baptist Theological Seminary. However, the public relations director for the seminary stated publicly that the Concerned Christians' post office box had been obtained "under false pretenses." [70]

Opposition, often more militant, continued during the eight-city tour. At the New York "Day of Hope" banquet in the Waldorf Astoria Hotel, five members of the International Workers Party (two of whom leaped onto chairs) attempted to disrupt the affair.[71] The following night, at Madison Square Garden, Rev. Moon invited those who opposed him to stand up and speak. Outside, more than a dozen groups ranging from Trotskyite and Marxist militants to "God's Umbrella" of Baptist, Methodist, and Nazarene groups demonstrated and passed out leaflets to the thousands who couldn't get in.[72]

Opposition tactics were rougher in Philadelphia. Phone lines were cut and the telephone company cut off service for the phone number listed on campaign posters after receiving an order to cancel the number; gas service to the Philadelphia center was cut off after the gas company received a phone call alerting them to a bogus gas leak in the building; and an unordered termite exterminator arrived at the center all equipped to fumigate.[73] In Washington, D.C., bricks were tossed through plate glass windows at campaign headquarters and van tires were slashed.[74]

However, more serious than specific incidents were mounting forms of institutional resistance. Problems with the U.S. Immigration and Naturalization Service surfaced during the thirty-two city tour. Initially having obtained six-month tourist visas for missionaries, the church's petition to have these visas altered was denied. In Salt Lake City, forty German IOWC members were apprehended by agents of the U.S. Immigration and Naturalization Service, charged with over-extension of their visas and given thirty days to leave the United States. By late 1974, 583 foreign members of the Unification Church were subject to deportation proceedings.[75] A second source of institutional resistance was the secular media. Here a combination of Rev. Moon's inaccessibility (no personal interviews were granted during tours) and complaints against the movement created a bad press.

Nevertheless, the most potentially serious source of organized resistance to the movement were families of converts. In Omaha, Nebraska, a sixteen-year-old member was subject to "deprogramming" and committed (without official record) by her mother to a local hospital for three weeks in late 1973.[76] In Des Moines, Iowa, a college student, after attending a weekend workshop, was committed by his parents to the psychiatric ward of a local hospital in early 1974.

The church responded to opposition in several ways. In Tarrytown, New York, the church sponsored public Fourth of July fireworks at Belvedere in both 1973 and 1974, attracting as many as 10,000 people.[77] During the Day of Hope Tours, movement spokesmen, PR teams, advertisements (including one full-page ad run in several cities entitled, "Have Christians Forsaken the Words of Jesus?") and letters were utilized to counter opposition. By May, 1974, these initiatives coalesced into a church public relations department. The movement's "War on Pornography" was a decidedly different approach to public relations adopted during the eight-city tour. More of a counter-offensive, 300-member marches on pornography districts in cities on the tour's itinerary generated publicity for speaking engagements while distracting attention from themselves.

For the most part, however, the movement was not overly concerned with criticism. Not only was there a lack of coordination among its critics but there was a lack of any underlying consensus that could unify a broad base of opposition. Left alone, fundamentalist Christians or Marxist protesters outside rallies generally ended up arguing against each other or among themselves. Thus, despite the severity of isolated attacks, opposition actually enhanced the movement's goal of public visibility. Another reason for the movement's lack of concern for outside criticism was its own success, the most substantial of which after Madison Square Garden was its eight-city Day of Hope stop in the Bay Area.

Success in San Francisco

Prospects for the eight-city Day of Hope tour stop in San Francisco, scheduled for December 9, 1974, were not initially promising. In Seattle, there were vocal pickets and a bomb threat. In San Francisco, the church's contract for use of the San Francisco Opera House was canceled in October by the Board of Trustees who were fearful of crowd turmoil. Threatened with a civil suit, the board relented but set down a stringent set of conditions. Among them were a $1 million insurance policy against personal injury or property damage; an agreement by the church to reserve the Civic Auditorium for the same night and to provide a closed circuit TV hookup, so the overflow crowd, if any, could hear the lecture; the provision of a security force; and the designation of a church staff of 350 persons for ushering and crowd control.[78]

Despite foreboding events and regulations, the San Francisco Day of Hope stop, according to Regional Director Paul Werner, was "the greatest success since Madison Square Garden." The December 7th kick-off banquet, again held at Benjamin Swig's Fairmont Hotel, brought out 1,160 San Franciscans. A letter of welcome from California Governor Ronald Reagan was read. Proclamations were announced from San Francisco, Berkeley, Oakland, San Leandro, Concord, Burlingame, San Mateo, Stockton, Menlo Park, and Hayward. The city of Oakland proclaimed December 9th as Sun Myung Moon Day and presented him with a tie tack and cuff links in the shape of an oak tree.[79] Rev. Moon noted, "I never expected such a heart-warming welcome in this golden state."[80]

The December 9, 1974, talk brought 5,000 people to the 3,200-seat San Francisco Opera House with the overflow directed to the Municipal Auditorium a block away. Although a full contingent of protestors including "street Christians," Amnesty International (which produced a flyer urging readers to ask South Korea's President Park about jailed religious leaders), the Christian World Liberation Front, and the International Workers' Party gathered outside, they were either drowned out by Paul Werner's marching band or at odds among themselves. According to one report, "The Christians were arguing against each other, calling each other Satan."[81] Inside, there were no disturbances during Rev. Moon's speech.

Far from worrying about external threats in the United States, the movement was planning to take its crusade overseas. Late 1974 was a harvest of sorts for the newly-emergent national movement. Summarizing advances made during its three-year period of total evangelism, American HSA-UWC President Neil Salonen, in a December, 1974 speech to members, noted,

> Three years ago, when Father [Rev. Moon] called us together into a Director's Conference, we had only a handful of members—less than 300! Since that time, we have seen what mighty things can be accomplished. Our movement has multiplied ten times, reaching almost three thousand by the end of this month. We have been catapulted from relative obscurity to national prominence, putting on projects worthy of groups many times our size. Now at last we can think in realistic terms of expanding to an international level.[82]

Based on the tour's success in America, Rev. Moon, on Thanksgiving day, announced plans for an international Day of Hope tour to begin in Japan, January 11, 1975. Earlier he had announced his intention of sending missionaries to 120 nations in the spring of 1975. Plans were made for expanded training programs at Barrytown and a future university. Consistent with the international thrust was the formation of a thirty-member United Nations PR team.

These initiatives, as well as membership goals and projected rallies at Yankee Stadium and the Washington Monument, were discussed at a director's conference in Los Angeles on December 21, 1974. Equally important was an event the previous day, when Rev. Moon presided over the blessing in marriage of Miss Onni Soo Lim, then director of the Oakland center, and Dr. Mose Durst, later to become the national president of the Unification Church in America. This ceremony inaugurated a new era in the Bay Area and national movement.

The Oakland Family

The new era launched in the Bay Area with the marriage of Soo Lim (Onni) and Dr. Mose Durst was that of 'The Oakland Family'. Initially a mission outpost of Mr. Choi's San Francisco-based Re-Education Foundation, the Oakland Family's membership totals skyrocketed from a handful of members to several hundred from 1972 to 1974. While existing Bay Area centers were depleted by the demands of national mobilization, the Oakland Family thrived and inherited both the Berkeley Center and what remained of Mr. Choi's Re-Education Foundation by the end of 1974.

In one sense, the Oakland Family emerged alongside of the national movement. However, it also was part of the national movement. At the December 21, 1974 directors' conference in Los Angeles which followed the Dursts' wedding and which effectively closed Reverend Moon's three year "Day of Hope" campaign in America, Onni (Soo Lim) Durst was appointed coordinator for California, excluding Los Angeles.

Its emergence alongside of yet part of the national movement would be the ruling dynamic of the Oakland Family's development after 1974. By combining techniques suited to the Bay Area with the level of intensity characteristic of the national movement, the Oakland Family achieved exceptional results. At the same time, by initiating its own programs, often with a less than clear articulation of their connection to the national movement, the Oakland Family sparked tensions within. In addition, the "time bomb" to which Reverend Moon had referred, exploded after 1975 in the form of media attacks, kidnappings, deprogrammings, court cases, and government investigations. To fully explore these dimensions in the emergence of the Unification Church is beyond the scope of this account.

NOTES

1. John Lofland, "Moonies in America: From Rag-tag Band to Streamlined Movement." Lecture given at the University of California at Davis, June 5, 1979.

2. David S.C. Kim, "Report on the Korean Missionary Conference," *United Temple Bulletin,* March 15, 1969.

3. Betsy Drapcho, "Word from Washington," *New Age Frontiers,* January 1972.

4. David S.C. Kim, "News Report: Washington, D.C.," *United Temple Bulletin,* January 1, 1972.

5. "Berkeley," *New Age Frontiers,* February 1972.

6. The Pioneers, "Pioneer Training Session, New York," *New Age Frontiers,* April 1972.

7. Ibid.

8. Rick Hunter, "Our Relationship to the True Parents," *New Age Frontiers,* April 1972.

9. Barbara Mikesell, "Three Weeks Pioneer Training in New York," *The Way of the World* , May 1972.

10. Farley Jones, "Notes on Family Meeting, March 16, 1972." Unpublished transcript of meeting in Washington, D.C.

11. Articles in the *Berkeley Gazette* included "Lectures by Moon Set," February 19, 1972; "Unification Berkeleyans Attend Meet," February 12, 1972; and "Unification Movement's Founder Here," March 8, 1972; the *Oakland Tribune* ran an article, "Ecumenist Speaks," March 5, 1972.

12. Farley Jones, "Notes on Family Meeting," March 16, 1972.

13. Rick Hunter, "Our Relationship to the True Parents," *New Age Frontiers,* April 1972.

14. David S.C. Kim, ed., "Origins and Growth of the One World Crusade in the USA," *Day of Hope in Review, part 1, 1972-1974,* (Tarrytown, New York: HSA-UWC, 1974), 2.

15. Farley Jones, "Notes on Family Meeting.", March 16, 1972

16. David S.C. Kim, "Marching Across this Great Land to Make it Free," *The Way of the World,* May 1972.

17. "One World Crusade Campaigns Throughout the United States of America," *The Way of the World,* July 1972.

18. David S.C. Kim, "The Establishment of HSA and My Role as One of the Participants,." *United Temple Bulletin*, May, 1970

19. See *The Way of the World*, May, July, and November 1972.

20. David S.C. Kim, "Mobile Unit II Moves West Coast States," *The Way of the World*, November 1972.

21. "New Strategy for the MFT: Divide and Conquer!" *New Hope News*, May 10, 1974

22. Regis Hanna, "Report on the National Director's Conference," *New Age Frontiers*, January 1971.

23. Farley Jones, "Notes on Family Meeting," March 16, 1972.

24. Young Oon Kim, *Memoirs, 1972.*

25. Ibid.

26. Louise Berry, "Latest Developments on Belvedere," *Pioneer's Progress*, September 10, 1972.

27. Interview with William and Leslie Cook at Berkeley, California, November 1978.

28. Louise Berry, "Latest Developments on Belvedere," *Pioneer's Progress*, September 10 1972.

29. Young Oon Kim, *Memoirs*, 1972.

30. "Belvedere Is Ours," and "At Belvedere," *Pioneer's Progress*, October 10, 1972.

31. "Permanent Mobile Fund-raising Team Begins Four Month Mission," *New Age Frontiers*, November 10, 1972.

32. Ibid.

33. John Hessel, "Report from New York," *New Age Frontiers*, February 1972.

34. Sun Myung Moon, "The Role of Unified Science in the Moral Orientation of the World," *New Age Frontiers*, December 8, 1972.

35. "Unified Science Conference," *New Age Frontiers*, December 8, 1972

36. Sun Myung Moon, "Safeguard the Unified Front," *Master Speaks*, December 31, 1971.

37. "Our Leader Meets President Thieu, U.S. Senators, Congressmen," *The Way of the World*, May 1973.

38. "Summary of the Third Pioneer Training Program," *New Age Frontiers*, December 30, 1972.

39. David S.C. Kim, "One World Crusade Progressing Rapidly in America," *The Way of the World*, April 1973.

40. Jonathan Slevin, "Report on the 100 Day International Training Session," *The Way of the World*, May 1973.

41. "American Family," *The Way of the World*, July 1973.

42. Ibid.

43. David S.C. Kim, *Day of Hope in Review*, part 1, vii.

44. "New Hope Comes to America," *The Way of the World*, September 1973.

45. David S.C. Kim, "One World Crusade Progressing Rapidly in America," *The Way of the World*, April 1973.

46. See David S.C. Kim, *Day of Hope in Review*, part 1, 62-160.

47. "Moon People Offer Hope," *The Daily Californian*, January 22, 1974.

48. "32-city Tour," *New Hope News*, May 10, 1974.

49. "Boston SMMCC Attendance Breaks All Records," *New Hope News*, July 25, 1974.

50. John M. Lovell, "Moon Terms Maine Handle to America," *Portland Press Herald*, February 16, 1974.

51. John Price, David Carlson, Leon Pine, "Titanium Factory Serves Modern Korea," *The Way of the World*, October 1973.

52. Michael Y. Warder, "Prospectus for the International Cultural Foundation," *The Way of the World*, January 1974.

53. "The Little Angels," *The Way of the World*, April 1973.

54. "Becoming International Leaders," *The Way of the World*, July/August 1974.

55. "Statement by the Rev. Sun Myung Moon: America in Crisis, Answer to Watergate, Forgive, Love, Unite," Official Statement, HSA-UWC, November 30, 1973.

56. "In Time of Crisis, Pray," *The Way of the World*, January 1974.

57. Sue Cronkite, "Cheering, Chanting Youths Prove Spirit of America Still Alive; Support Nixon," *Birmingham News*, December 24, 1973.

58. Laurence Stern and William R. MacKaye, "Rev. Moon: Nixon Backer," *Washington Post*, February 15, 1974.

59. Joy Schmidt, "Three Days at the Capitol," *The Way of the World*, July/August 1974.

60. Art Buchwald, "God Doesn't Want Nixon Impeached," *Daily News*, July 27, 1974.

61. Neil Salonen, "Providential Perspective," *New Hope News*, July 25, 1974.

62. "A Garden Attraction," *New York Times*, September 22, 1974.

63. "Sun Myung Moon, Prophet to Thousands, Stirs Waves of Controversy as He Prepares for Big Rally Here," *New York Times*, September 16, 1974.

64. "Thousands Crowd Garden to Hear Speech by Moon," *New York Times*, September 19, 1974.

65. "The Messiah—The Last Hope for Mankind," *The Way of the World*, September/October 1974.

66. David S.C. Kim, "Eight City Tour," *Day of Hope in Review*, part 2, 320-517; see also "Capsule: Day of Hope 1974," *The Way of the World*, January 1975.

67. Sun Myung Moon, "The Significance of MSG," *Master Speaks*, September 19, 1974; also "The Messiah--The Last Hope of Mankind," *The Way of the World*, September/October 1974.

68. "Students Oppose Moon," *Oakland Tribune*, January 20, 1974. The coalition included the Chinese Christian Fellowship, Inter-Varsity Christian Fellowship, Resurrection City, Baptist Student Ministries, Christian World Liberation Front, Campus Crusade for Christ and Forever Family Ministries.

69. Laurence Stern and William R. MacKaye, "Enigmatic Rev. Moon Works Economic Miracles," *Washington Post*, February 15, 1974.

70. The church exposed the document in a letter by Neil Albert Salonen mailed to 2,000 ministers in the last 19 cities of the 32-city tour. See *New Hope News*, May 10, 1974.

71. "Church Hosts Swank Bash," *The Daily News*, Tarrytown, New York, September 18, 1974.

72. "Rev. Moon and His Adherents Facing Wrath of Evangelists," *The Daily News*, September 14, 1974; "Sun Myung Moon, Prophet to Thousands, Stirs Waves of Controversy as he Prepares for Big Rally Here," *New York Times*, September 16, 1974.

73. "Philadelphia Day of Hope: Victory Despite Persecution," *New Hope News*, October 7, 1974.

74. "The Campaign," *New Hope News*, October 21, 1974.

75. "A U.S. Agency's Act May Eclipse Crusade of Sun Myung Moon," *The Wall Street Journal*, September 20, 1974.

76. Jill Criesing, "NCLU Probes 'Programmed' Girl's Plight," *Dundee Sun*, [Omaha, Nebraska] November 15, 1973; "Girl, 16, Happy to Resume Living at Church," *Dundee Sun*, November 22, 1974; "Family Major Point of Unification Leader," *Omaha World Herald*, November 26, 1974.

77. "Unification Church to Celebrate on 4th," *The Daily News,* [Tarrytown, New York] July 3, 1974; "Belvedere Hosts 10,000 on July 4th," *The Way of the World*, July/August 1974; "Father Speaks to 10,000 Guests on 4th of July," *New Hope News*, July 20, 1974.

78. "Evangelist Back at Opera House," *San Francisco Chronicle*, November 9, 1974.

79. David S.C. Kim, *Day of Hope in Review*, part 2, 447.

80. Joy Schmidt, "Crowd Overflows in San Francisco," *New Hope News* , December 23, 1974.

81. Ibid.

82. Neil Salonen, "Looking Ahead . . ." *New Hope News*, December 23, 1974.